THE PARENT GUIDE TO

PARENT AND CHILD SEX TALKS

WHY, WHEN, AND HOW

TO TELL YOUR KIDS ABOUT SEXUAL HEALTH

Raising Sexually and Relationships Smart Kids

BY

DR. KWAME FRIMPONG

**Foreword By Pastor Dickson Sarpong
(ICGC Jesus Temple)**

www.kflifecoaching.com
www.LetsLoveRight.com
Email. Drkwamefrimpong@gmail.com
Whatsapp. 011233 024 755 9692

Endorsements

The topic of sex education is essential and often neglected by parents. Many parents avoid the topic or approach it feeling shame. Many times, they simply don't know how to start and continue the dialogue. Dr. Frimpong goes right into the heart of the conversation. He gives straightforward information about talking to your children about God's gift of sex without making it feel awkward or uncomfortable. This is a valuable resource for parents and soon-to-be parents, and it owns a place in the church library

John C. Thomas, Ph.D., Ph.D.

Professor
Licensed Professional Counselor (LPC-S. VA)
Certified Substance Abuse Counselor (CSAC, VA)
Certified Sex Therapist (CST)
Certified Sex Addiction Therapist (CSAT)
Certified Partner Trauma Therapist (CPTT)

Parents have long been searching for guidance on how to address the sensitive topics of sexuality and relationships with their children. In today's world, where peers and online content increasingly influence children, it has become more essential than ever to approach these subjects thoughtfully and effectively.

Now, the wait is over. Dr. Kwame Frimpong's new book, based on years of research, provides parents with a clear, well-researched guide on engaging in meaningful and open conversations with their children about these often-taboo topics. This book is a must-read for every parent who wants to navigate the complexities of raising informed, respectful, and responsible young people.

Bishop Frank Ofosu Appiah
The general overseer of Living Springs Fellowship International
Pastor of All Nations USA, Atlanta, Ga

Teens in North America are faced with new challenges that were not at the forefront 30 years ago.

Unfortunately, parents lack the resources to help address the areas around human sexuality. This book will act as a guidepost for any parent desiring to teach and engage their child on difficult topics like sex through the biblical lens. Not only will the reader be well informed about the realities of raising children in today's world, but you will also be fully equipped with actionable steps on how to teach and carry out conversations revolving around sex with young people in your life.

We do not doubt that this book will equip the body of Christ to stand firm against the war that rages on against our human souls. As you read the pages of this book, we are confident that you will find within it the strategies necessary to raise children to love their God and appreciate all that he has made, inclusive of sex.

Pastor Ken and Rosa Ononeze.
Calvary Worship Center New Westminster

Dr. Frimpong is not just a colleague; I consider him a friend and scholar with deep insight and knowledge as a clinical mental health practitioner. His scholarship in the area of guiding the development of children from the context of healthy sexual development and relationships is a significant contribution to the profession. Parenting is a divine assignment because of the divine nature of the human body. As we guide the physical, intellectual, and psycho-social development of our children, parents must also attend to the development of healthy sexuality in children. It is as if this area of development has been off-limits to the wisdom and guidance of parents. Just as the healthy functioning of the brain can predetermine the pathways of a child's future, healthy sexual development, and relationships are equally important in fostering growth and development. I am excited that Dr. Kwame Frimpong has provided parents with such a valuable guide to assist them with fostering healthy sexual development in their children as parents successfully fulfill their divine assignment.

Dr. Philicia Jefferson, Ph.D., D.Min, LPC, CRC

Founder, NCCI Counseling Services & Training Inc

Dr. Kwame Frimpong's book is an invaluable resource for parents and educators seeking to navigate the sensitive yet crucial conversations surrounding sexuality and relationships. With profound insight and cultural awareness, he offers practical tools for fostering open dialogue and healthy development in young people. This work is a must-read for anyone committed to empowering the next generation with knowledge, confidence, and integrity."

— Dr. Clifton R. Clarke, Bishop, Professor, and Author

Dr. Kwame is passionate about educating parents and teens about godly and healthy sexuality. In an age of cultural relativism, Christians must return to God's view on sexuality and restore sexual purity. While sexuality can be a very difficult topic for Christians to discuss, if we don't teach our kids about this topic, someone else will. Dr. Kwame helps parents take back their God-given responsibility to train their children in godly values.

Justin Harley, PhD, LPC

Senior Pastor, Trinity Chapel

Assistant Professor of Clinical Counseling, Pentecostal Theological Seminary

Due to sexual silence and cultural taboos, sex education has long been a difficult subject for families. As a result, children often turn to peers and the internet for answers, leaving them vulnerable to misinformation. Dr. Kwame Frimpong's research-based resources provide much-needed guidance for parents to address these critical topics confidently and clearly. This material is essential in helping families navigate the complexities of sexuality and ensuring that children receive accurate, healthy information.

Apostle Elvis Acheampong
Gateway International Christian Church
Alexandria, VA

Acknowledgments

First and foremost, I give thanks to the Lord Jesus Christ, whose grace and guidance have empowered me to write with cultural relevance and academic insight. Without His unwavering presence, this work would not have been possible.

To my beloved wife, Mary—thank you for your constant support, love, dedication, and companionship. Your encouragement has been a source of strength and inspiration throughout this journey.

I am deeply grateful to Dr. Thomas of Liberty University, whose passion for educating society on the significance of sexuality and sex education has inspired me to address this vital issue in a culture that often remains silent on the matter.

I would also like to express my heartfelt appreciation to Pastor Dickson Sarpong and Dr. Frank Ofosu Appiah for their ongoing support and encouragement. Your belief in this project has been invaluable.

Lastly, I want to thank all my pastor friends, whose prayers and words of encouragement have provided the motivation I needed to bring this book to life.

Table of Contents

Endorsements.. iii

Acknowledgments.. ix

Foreword xv

Introduction.. xxi

Chapter 1: The Gift of sexuality.. 1

The Gift of Human Sexuality 2

Marriage as a Reflection of God's Love for His Children 4

Sexual Brokenness: The Impact of Sin on Human Sexuality............. 5

The Family's Role in Sexuality.. 7

The Gift of Sex 9

Chapter 2: Consequences of inadequate sex education from Home ... 15

Seeking Information from Reliable Sources 15

Adolescents Feeling Unprepared to Make Informed Decisions...... 18

Peer Influence on Boys' Sexual Education 18

Media as a Dominant Source of Sexual Information 19

Shyness and Shame 19

Low Self-Esteem... 20

Chapter 3: Why start early.. 21

Pre-Adolescence: A Critical and Curious Period.............. 21

Sex Education from School is not enough 23

Sex Education: An Essential Component of Adolescent
Development 24

Competing with Peers: The Impact of Delayed Sex Education....... 25

The Importance of Timing in Sex Education 26

Chapter 4: The importance of parent-child sexual health and relationship education 28

Sexuality and Early Curiosity 28

The Importance of Early Conversations about Sexuality 29

The Serious Ramifications of a Lack of Sexual Health Education ...30

Adolescents Feel Unprepared 31

Chapter 5: Youth challenges in discussing sexuality and relationships with parents 35

Sexuality Education: What Does This Imply? 35

Sexuality Education in Australia 36

Desire for Parental Communication 37

What Adolescents Hear and What They Really Want to Hear 40

Adolescents Often Hear Warnings 40

The Feeling of Unpreparedness 42

Emotional Barriers: Discomfort and Embarrassment 42

Gender Dynamics in Communication 43

Impact of Inadequate Communication 44

Chapter 6: Young Boys Receive Little Sex Education 46

The Role of Parents in Sex Education 47

Peer Influence on Sexual Education 48

Media as a Dominant Source of Sexual Information 49

High-Risk Sexual Behaviors 49

Difficulty Seeking Help Due to Sexual Silence and Shame 50

Self-Esteem Issues 50

Addressing Cultural and Societal Barriers 51

Encouraging Parental Involvement 51

Chapter 7: Parents are the best source 53

Parents and caregivers serve as the foundation for children's sexual development 53

Reducing Sexual Risk during Adolescence 55

Parents as Primary Sexual Socializing Agents 56

Increasing Understanding of Sexual Relationship Development ... 57

Making Informed Decisions 58

Helping Young People Overcome Peer Pressure 58

Developing Positive Attitudes and Beliefs on Sexuality 59

Emotional Support and Sexual Health 60

The Challenges of the Parent-Child "Sex Talk" 61

Myth that Children Will Act Out 61

Chapter 8: The Issues in Same-Gender Communication: Mothers Talk to Daughters, and Fathers Talk To Sons 66

The Importance of Open Communication About Sex 66

The Real Issue 68

Chapter 9: Barriers, Culture taboos, sexual silence, Communication, and shyness 71

Why Is It So Difficult to Teach Sexual Health to Our Children? 71

Parent-Child Gender Barriers 73

Lack of Knowledge or Parental Uncertainty 74

Overcoming Barriers to Effective Parent-Child Communication .. 74

Sexual Shame as a Barrier 75

Culture as a Barrier 76

Sexual Silence, Cultural Taboo, and Religiosity Contributing to Shame 77

Challenges in Menstruation Communication 78

Lack of Knowledge or Parental Uncertainty 79

Chapter 10: How to offer sexual health and relationship education (iCREATE) Method..81

Guide for Parents to Discuss "The Sex Talk" with Their Kids 81

Misconception of Sex Education 83

The Current State of Sex Education................................84

Traditional Gender Roles..86

Let's Talk About the Guide 86

Emotional Support and Sexual Health 90

Chapter 11: Teaching your teenagers to build healthy relationships 102

The Importance of Healthy Communication 102

Sexual Coercion: Traumatic Impacts 110

From Toddler to Preadolescence......................................144

Addressing Challenges and Concerns 152

Conclusion..158

About the Author..164

References..166

Foreword

It is both an honor and a privilege to write this foreword for my dear friend, Dr. Kwame Frimpong, whose doctoral studies in the counseling profession have led him to publish his thought-provoking and essential book, *"The Parent and Child Sex Talks: Raising Sexually and Relationship-Smart Kids."* This book arrives at a critical juncture in our society—one where the rapid changes in technology and culture present unprecedented challenges for families. As a society, we are waking up to the reality that discussions about sexual health and relationships are not just important—they are necessary for the well-being of our children.

You will agree with me that the culture many of us grew up in did not emphasize open conversations about sexual health. This was largely due to cultural taboos and what I often refer to as "sexual silence." In our homes and even within our churches, such topics were often avoided, and as a result, we were left with limited knowledge and the inability to have healthy, informed conversations about our bodies, relationships, and boundaries. Unfortunately, the silence surrounding these critical topics continues to persist in many communities today. However, in the modern world, our children are bombarded by sexual distortion, primarily through the internet, social media, and peer pressure. They are exposed to distorted images of sex, often without the maturity or guidance needed to process this information. If we, as parents and caregivers, do not empower ourselves to engage with our children on these subjects, they are at great risk of being influenced by harmful and misleading sources.

Dr. Kwame Frimpong has created a much-needed resource to help parents navigate this challenging terrain. The Parent and Child Sex Talks serves as a practical and compassionate guide for parents, church leaders, educators, and even school systems. It equips them with the tools to engage in open, honest, and age-appropriate conversations about sexual health. Dr. Frimpong's approach is holistic—combining biblical principles with research-based findings. His ability to merge these two perspectives makes this book especially valuable to individuals and organizations within faith-based communities who seek to educate young people on sexuality in a way that is both spiritually sound and scientifically informed. This book offers a balanced approach that recognizes the importance of spiritual guidance while also embracing the need for practical strategies rooted in research and evidence-based practices.

Dr. Frimpong's work goes beyond simply providing information; it offers actionable techniques that will empower parents, grandparents, and church leaders to break the silence and initiate healthy dialogues with their children. Drawing from his extensive background in counseling and family therapy, he offers clear, concrete methods to help adults approach sensitive topics in a way that fosters trust and openness. This is not a one-time conversation, but rather an ongoing dialogue that should evolve as children grow and mature. Dr. Frimpong provides a step-by-step approach for approaching these discussions at various stages of a child's development, ensuring that parents are not only equipped to address sexual health, but also relationship dynamics, emotional intelligence, and the complexities of consent and respect.

Furthermore, the book offers valuable insights into how parents and leaders can create environments in which children feel safe to ask questions and express concerns without fear of judgment. Dr. Frimpong emphasizes that these conversations should be rooted in love and respect, making it clear that healthy sexual education is about fostering a positive, holistic understanding of self-worth and dignity. He helps readers understand that this work is not just about protecting children from harm, but also about empowering them to make informed decisions about their bodies, their relationships, and their future.

In a world where sexual misinformation is rampant and the pressures on young people are ever-growing, The Parent and Child Sex Talks is a beacon of hope. It provides the guidance, wisdom, and encouragement that parents and leaders need to confidently address the sexual and relational health of the next generation. This book is an invaluable resource for anyone serious about raising children who are not only sexually informed, but also emotionally intelligent, respectful, and capable of forming healthy, meaningful relationships. I highly recommend it to parents, caregivers, church leaders, and educators who are looking for a comprehensive, practical, and biblically grounded resource to help them navigate the challenges of modern-day parenting. Dr. Kwame Frimpong has done a tremendous service by producing work that will undoubtedly have a lasting, positive impact on children, families, and communities for generations to come

As we move forward into an increasingly complex world, we must equip our children with the knowledge and tools to make informed decisions about their sexual health and relationships. Dr. Kwame Frimpong's book is an essential resource for anyone looking to take proactive steps in raising responsible, respectful, and empowered children. It serves as a vital tool for breaking down the walls of silence and stigma that have traditionally surrounded these conversations, ensuring that future generations are better prepared to navigate the challenges of a rapidly changing world. With his profound expertise and dedication to the well-being of young people, Dr. Frimpong has created a resource that will undoubtedly leave a legacy in the lives of parents, children, and communities alike.

Pastor Dickson Sarpong

(ICGC Jesus Temple)

Introduction

Congratulations! By opening this book, you have taken an important step towards raising sexually and relationship-smart kids.

Perhaps you have noticed your 10-year-old encountering inappropriate content online, and it is quite alarming. Maybe your 7-year-old has started asking, "What does sex mean?" and you are struggling to find the right words to answer. Or perhaps your 12-year-old is engaged in sexting, and trying to discuss it only leads to arguments.

You are not alone. As a concerned parent, you worry about your children's understanding of sex, sexual health, romantic relationships, peer influence, and the negative impacts of today's society. In our world, sexual issues, high-risk behaviors, and internet safety are significant concerns affecting young people. The challenges related to sexual matters are real, and many parents feel lost in how to address them.

Before graduate school, I would not say I knew anything about parent-child sex talks. Being an immigrant who was raised in a cultural background of sexual silence, cultural taboos, and shame associated with sexually related conversation, parent-child sex talks are a no-no. The discomfort, shyness and not knowing what to say would be impossible to talk with my children. I faced a lot of barriers including communication barriers, cultural barriers, gender barriers, etc.

However, that changed when I took a course on human sexuality. God opened my eyes to see that as a parent I should be the person my child goes to for anything related to sexuality and relationship skills. I decided to embark on a journey, a mission that will give hope and empowerment to parents so they can help their children- the next generation after God. This journey led me to my research interest- human sexuality.

This book was in part published from my dissertation. Twenty (20) parents from five countries and cultural backgrounds reside in the USA. They shared their struggles, barriers, and the need for such a book. Based on my research findings, I saw that most parents have the same desire, in this sexually saturated society, how do we prepare our children with godly values? Well, that is the goal of this book. Thirdly, I wrote the book based on the parenting challenge I witnessed in my clinical work. As a licensed professional counselor, I counsel parents and young people a lot, and one huge barrier is home-based sex education,

Before entering graduate school, my understanding of parent-child conversations about sex was minimal. As an immigrant, I grew up in a cultural environment steeped in the silence surrounding sexuality, where taboos and shame cloaked any discussion of sexual topics. The thought of having such conversations with my children felt daunting—overwhelmed by discomfort, shyness, and uncertainty about what to say. I encountered numerous barriers, including communication hurdles, cultural obstacles, and gender expectations.

However, everything changed when I enrolled in a course on human sexuality. This experience opened my eyes to the crucial role I, as a parent, should play in guiding my children through discussions about sexuality and relationship skills. The insights I gained inspired me to write this book, which is partly derived from my dissertation.

In my research, I engaged with twenty parents from five different countries and diverse cultural backgrounds, all of whom now reside in the USA. They candidly shared their struggles, barriers, and the pressing need for resources like this book. My findings revealed a common desire among parents: in today's sexually saturated society, how can we equip our children with godly values? This book aims to address that very challenge, offering guidance and support for parents navigating these vital conversations

Here are some similar concerns that many parents share:

- **Parent:** "My boy is losing interest in real-life activities. I am very worried; the internet is good, but it can also be very bad sometimes."

- **Parent:** "The internet is making children very emotional and unrealistic about the practical world."

- **Parent:** "Children are becoming less interested in family time and other social gatherings. This will affect our family values and bonds."

- **Parent:** "They don't like to come out of their room—their own world. They avoid socializing with family members or our friends when they visit. Sometimes, they don't even say 'hi' or 'hello' to family friends and relatives. It often seems like they don't know what to say or how to talk to their friends or relatives."

- **Parent:** "Children are copying unethical behavior from online friends and dangerous online groups. They are following inappropriate cultures, exposed to violent games and activities, and watching inappropriate content like photos and movies on terrorism and radicalization. They are not learning good things."

- **Parent:** "Whatever they see, they internalize. So, while they are using the internet and we are not keeping an eye on them, they might be watching something very violent, which may develop violent tendencies in their minds."

- **Parent:** "They are spending too much time on the internet and are getting addicted. I would say they are addicted to the internet and social media, which affects them both emotionally and physically."

Here is a brief self-assessment to gauge your level of comfort when initiating conversations about sexual topics with your child/children:

1. Do you feel at ease when initiating communication with your child/children on sexually related topics?

2. Do you feel comfortable talking to your children about sexual health matters?

3. Do you experience feelings of awkwardness whenever you try to initiate a conversation about sexual topics with your children?

4. Is there a level of shame associated with initiating sexual health conversations with your children?

5. Do you have the confidence to discuss these topics openly and effectively?

Here is the good news: Parents are still the best source of sex education for their children according to studies, and this book will equip you to help your children effectively.

The Parent and Child Sexual Talks Workbook was developed with a robust research background to address these concerns. Alongside the "Raising Sexually Smart Children Workshop," this book provides pointers, tips, tools, and resources to help you navigate these important conversations.

This workbook will help parents to:

- **Technical Know-How:** Gain the technical know-how to engage their children in open and honest communication about sexual health.

- **Create a Safe Space:** Establish a supportive and non-judgmental environment for discussing sexual matters with ease.

- **Increase Comfort Level:** Enhance their own comfort level with home-based sex education.

- **Improve Children's Comfort:** Help children feel more comfortable sharing their sexual struggles with their parents.

- **Reduce Shame:** Diminish the shame associated with initiating conversations about sexual topics for both parents and children.

- **Become a Go-To Resource:** Encourage children to see their parents as their primary resource for all their sexual health needs.

While this book focuses on pre-teens, You can use it for children from the 6 year olds.

Dr. Kwame Frimpong

PhD, Counselor Educator and Researcher

Atlanta GA

The Age of Sexual Temptation:

Teens Are Having Sex Too Fast!

Starting sex education too late has significant consequences for adolescents. By the time many parents begin these conversations, their children may already be under the influence of their peers, who can provide misleading or incomplete information. As such, the timing of sex education is crucial. Experts recommend that parents start these conversations early and take advantage of "teachable moments" as they arise in the child's life, regardless of age. Early and ongoing discussions can help children develop a healthy understanding of sex and relationships before they are exposed to external influences. However, many parents still view sex education as a one-time talk that should happen only when their children reach adolescence. This outdated notion often results in missed opportunities to build a foundation of knowledge and values that can guide adolescents through their formative years.

Statistics:

- Sexual behavior is starting at a younger age, and oral and anal sex has become almost normalized among 13-year-olds.

- Young people now have a greater number of sexual partners than their parents did.

- Children are growing up in a highly sexualized cultural environment.

- 55% of adolescents become sexually active by 18 years of age.

- Approximately 1 in 5 15-year-olds and 2 in 3 18-year-olds report having had sexual intercourse.

- A survey report indicated that about 42.7% of Ghanaian girls and 26.6% of boys become sexually active in their teens.

- A 2004 nationally representative survey in Ghana indicated that nearly 75% of sexually active adolescent girls and 33% of sexually active boys reported receiving money or gifts in exchange for sex.

Christian and Sexual Values

- Recent statistics show that many Christians have replaced biblical standards with fleshly desires.

- Christians are increasingly willing to follow cultural trends (e.g., Christian Mingle & JDate).

- 61% of Christians said they would have sex before marriage.

- 56% said it's appropriate to cohabitate after dating for 6 months to 2 years.

Danger Zone: Learning From the Wrong Places

- 74% of teens say friends and TV are major sources of information about sex.

- Only 10% of teens say their parents provided more information.

Pre-Teen Sexual Behavior, Sexting, and Mental Health

- 60% of 18-19-year-olds have had oral sex.

- In a study of youth aged 14-24, 24% of those who sent nude images or messages were 14-17 years old.

- In one study of 606 high school students, approximately 18% of boys and 17% of girls sent sexually suggestive or nude photo messages.

- 46% of high school students report having had sex, with 5.9% doing so before age 13.

- By age 20, 75% have had premarital sex.

Youth Lack of Relationship Skills Has a Cost

- According to a study done by York University, 20% of teens reported being in a relationship by the age of 11.6, and 55% by the age of 12.9.

- By age 18, it is estimated that 95% of teens will have experience in romantic relationships.

- Teens aged 15-17 are almost twice as likely as those aged 13-14 to have had some type of romantic relationship experience.

Teen Pregnancy

- Annually, 16 million births occur to young women aged 15-19 years, representing 11% of all births.

- Approximately 2.5 million births occur to girls aged 12-15 years in low-resource countries each year, with around a million births to girls younger than 16 years in Africa.

- Early childbearing is linked with higher maternal mortality and morbidity rates.

- Complications with childbearing and maternal issues are the leading cause of death among adolescent females.

Sexual Abuse

- Traumatized children may feel powerless to open up and discuss their ordeals.

- One out of every three teens will experience an abusive or unhealthy relationship.

- One in three girls in the US is a victim of physical, emotional, or verbal abuse from a dating partner, a rate that far exceeds other types of youth violence.

Young People Wish Parents Taught Them

- One out of every three youths said they would like to know more about how to talk to a romantic partner regarding setting sexual boundaries.

- Young people would most prefer to talk about sex with their parents (72%), followed by friends (68%) and the internet (61%) (Marie Stopes International, 2008).

The Consequences of Delaying the Talk

- Parents compete with friends and social media when they delay parent-child sex talks.

Porn is Destroying Young People

- The age of first exposure to porn is 8.

- By the time children reach age 13, about 54% have watched porn, with 41% doing so during the school day.

- More children under the age of 16 are seeing pornography than at any other time.

- Sexual behavior is starting at a younger age, and oral and anal sex have become almost normalized among 13-year-olds.

- Young people now have a greater number of sexual partners than their parents did.

- Pornography is often viewed by young people as a source for sexual exploration, understanding sexual identities, and a form of sexual play, as well as a source of sexual education.

- Watching porn has mental consequences, including lack of concentration, risky behavior, shame, depression, anxiety, identity issues, and poor grades in school.

STDs

- In the US, youths account for almost half of the 18.9 million new cases of STIs each year.

Parents Are the Best Sex Educators According to Research

- Effective parent-child communication is paramount to building a child's sense of self-worth.

- Teens who receive sex education from their parents are more likely to resist pressure to engage in sexual risk behaviors than their peers who do not receive such education.

- Father absenteeism is linked to teens' sexually risky behaviors and pregnancy.

- When parents offer sex education to their children, it reduces sexual risk behaviors.

- Parent-child talks enhance children's self-esteem.

- African males are less likely to discuss sexuality with their parents.

- In cultures where conversations on sexuality and sexual health are forbidden, many girls and young women face shock when they reach puberty.

- Some refugee women report that they did not know about menstruation prior to menarche and only learned about pregnancy when they became pregnant with their first child.

The School System is Not the Best Source

- Although many public school systems offer educational programs on sexual health and sexuality (Hall et al., 2019), many students are not getting much-needed guidance and support from their parents.

Lack of Accurate Sexual Information

- A majority of young people in Africa have woefully inaccurate knowledge of sexuality.

- Poor sexuality knowledge is a major reason why the triple tragedy of HIV/AIDS, unwanted teenage pregnancy, and unsafe induced abortion continues to have its highest number of victims among young people on the continent.

- Children often rely on equally uninformed and ignorant peers for their education and information on sexuality.

To address these challenges, parents need to start sex education early, teaching how God view sex, engage in ongoing and open discussions, and build their competence and confidence in addressing sexual matters. By doing so, they can provide their children with the knowledge and support they need to make informed and healthy decisions about their sexual health.

Chapter 1

The Gift of sexuality

Human sexuality is one area that has been greatly damaged by the fall. Because of sin, humanity continues to suffer from sexual dysfunctions and sexual sins, including homosexuality. Portrayals of sexual behavior in televised media, such as pornography, same-sex marriage, and premarital sex, plague society. Unfortunately, these sexual behaviors are not how God intended sexuality to be.

Teenagers are being bombarded with pornography on the internet, luring them into sexual sins. Society's views on sexuality are constantly changing, encompassing various perspectives on sexuality, marriage, sexual orientation, and more. These secular views are infiltrating the church, and the body of Christ's inability to provide biblical, godly education about sexuality contributes to the struggle. It is crucial that

Christians understand God's intentions for this precious gift of sexuality.

The lack of biblical teaching and awareness about sexuality within the body of Christ, as God intended, opens the door for sexual distortions and sins.

The Gift of Human Sexuality

Sexuality is a creation of God, intended to be celebrated within the sacred covenant relationship between a husband and a wife. It is a means for a husband and wife to express their love for each other. God's plan for marriage involves the man and his wife becoming one flesh. As Moses stated, "Therefore shall a man leave his father and his mother and shall cleave unto his wife: and they shall be one flesh" (Genesis 2:24 NKJV). The idea of becoming one flesh refers to sexual intercourse (Penner & Penner, 2005). Sex is a gift from God.

When God created Adam and Eve, He made them sexual beings. As Rosenau and Wilson (2006) explain, "Sexuality also includes our general sexual desire and gender makeup, masculine and feminine" (p. 7). Sexuality is one of the most beautiful gifts God gave to His children. Rosenau (2002) beautifully describes sex as "glorious, innocent celebration lived out with instinctual honesty, respect, and zest for life" (p. 4).

It is high time that Christians begin teaching their children about the beauty of sexuality. Christians are called to follow God's teachings and impart this understanding to their children.

Intimacy

Sex also has a profound spiritual meaning. God intended the intimacy between married couples to demonstrate His love for His children. The unconditional love that a husband has for his wife serves as an illustration of God's own love for humanity. This love is meant to be without shame or fear, as described in Genesis: "And they were both naked, the man and his wife, and were not ashamed" (Genesis 2:25 NKJV). This scripture indicates that true, unconditional love between a man and his wife involves no shame or fear. It is an experience of unselfish love for each other.

The Holman Bible Dictionary beautifully describes sex as "for the procreation of children, the enhancement of the one-flesh relationship, and the pleasure of the married couple whose love can be nourished thereby" (p. 1252).

Paul sheds light on the love relationship between a husband and his wife in his letter to the Ephesians: "Husbands, love your wives, just as Christ also loved the church and gave Himself for her, that He might sanctify and cleanse her with the washing of water by the word" (Ephesians 5:25-26 NKJV).

Marriage as a Reflection of God's Love for His Children

Another practical example of how God uses the love between a husband and wife to demonstrate His unconditional love for His children is found in the book of Hosea. God commanded Hosea to marry a prostitute and show his love for her, as recorded: "Then the Lord said to me, 'Go again, love a woman who is loved by a lover and is committing adultery, just like the love of the Lord for the children of Israel, who look to other gods and love the raisin cakes of the pagans'" (Hosea 3:1 NKJV). The story of Hosea is a compelling picture of God's unconditional love, forgiveness, and never-ending faithfulness toward His covenant people. This proves that the love between married couples is meant to be a reflection of God's love for His children.

God designed sex as a way for couples to know each other on a deeper level. Genesis 4:1 reads, "And Adam knew Eve his wife; and she conceived and bore Cain, and said, 'I have gotten a man from the Lord.'" God designed sexuality for couples to express themselves more intimately and deeply. It is a means to consummate the marriage. Penner & Penner (2005) explain the Hebrew word "know" in this way: "the Hebrew word to know in Genesis 4:1 refers to sexual intercourse, and it is the same word that is used about knowing God; it is also a word for the genitals" (p. 29). Sexuality involves the spirit, soul, and body. It is three-dimensional (Rosenau, 2002).

Whenever one has sex with another person, they become one in spirit, soul, and body. As described by Paul, "Or do you not know that he who is joined to a harlot is one body with her? For the two, He says, 'shall become one flesh'" (1 Corinthians 6:16 NKJV). Paul explained that sexual union affects a person physically and emotionally. He wanted the church in Corinth to understand that they cannot just have sex with anyone other than their spouse. In other words, sex outside of marriage has consequences. Sexual intimacy was designed by God for a man and a woman who have entered a covenant relationship. It was not meant for people outside of holy matrimony. However, when humanity fell because of sin, everything was damaged, including sexuality.

Sexual Brokenness: The Impact of Sin on Human Sexuality

When Adam and Eve sinned against God, human sexuality was marred by the Fall. Humanity began practicing behaviors contrary to God's plan. The sexual brokenness that resulted from sin led to various sexual sins, including pornography, fornication, bestiality, lust, and other actions that go against the word of God. As noted by Mohler (2015):

"Sexual sin continues to plague society, and it must be remembered that the early church fathers contributed to the negative view of sexuality."

Instead of teaching that God designed sexuality as something beautiful and as a gift, early church teachings often portrayed sexuality as dirty.

These teachings greatly hurt the church and negatively impacted views on sexuality. One key church father who propagated this teaching was Augustine. Before his conversion, Augustine struggled with his own sexual issues, which influenced his views on sexuality. For example, he believed that sexual intercourse was the means through which original sin was transferred (Jones, 2004). His misunderstanding of sexuality led to sexual perversion. As noted by Jones (2004):

"This understanding of the sexual-spiritual nexus led Augustine, and those in the church who later adopted his theology, to emphasize the immaterial to such a degree that human sexuality was neglected and distorted" (p. 5).

Over time, the church did not adequately teach sexual wholeness as God intended. It is time for the church to address the issue of sexual sins, including homosexuality, with a balanced perspective. As the church preaches the unadulterated word of God in truth, the Holy Spirit's role is to convict the world of sin. However, Christians must speak up in love and not remain silent. As indicated by Schrock (2014):

"Older evangelicals seem mainly to be ignoring the problem, and younger evangelicals seem mainly to be attracted by accommodationists like David Gushee and Jim Wallis. Sadly, both are failing the greatest challenge of our day" (p. 9).

The church must begin to teach about sexual wholeness and God's original design for human sexuality, addressing sexual brokenness with compassion and biblical truth.

The Family's Role in Sexuality

God holds the Christian family responsible for teaching children about His ways, including sexuality. The family is the primary place where children learn about their own sexuality. If the family fails to provide this education, children will turn to friends, schools, and social media, where they may receive ungodly information. Additionally, if there are sexual sins within the family, children may repeat these sins in their own lives. For example, victims of sexual abuse can sometimes become abusers themselves. Proeve and Reilly (2007) state, "Craissati and McClurg (1996) found that approximately 50% of convicted child sexual abusers were themselves sexually abused." It is within the family that children learn about sexual purity. Balswick and Balswick (1989) emphasize, "Because the meaning of sexuality is learned within the social context, it is imperative that the family and community powerfully live out and communicate God's design for human sexuality" (p. 220).

The family environment provides a conducive atmosphere for children to learn who they are. The responsibility for parents to train their children was first given to Abraham. Genesis 18:19 (NKJV) states, "For

I have known him, in order that he may command his children and his household after him, that they keep the way of the Lord, to do righteousness and justice, that the Lord may bring to Abraham what He has spoken to him." When children are well-taught about God's ways, it positively affects society. God designed the family to uphold His ways from generation to generation. Proverbs 22:6 reminds us, "Train up a child in the way he should go, and when he is old he will not depart from it."

As the church engages in the battle over sexuality, it must not give up. The church cannot allow secular definitions of sexuality to dictate its path. Stewart (2003) notes, "Only by considering the Word of God can we understand our true purpose and identity. The world could never offer a true picture of the reasons for human existence" (p. 19). Satan will do everything in his power to redefine sexuality, morality, and marriage. However, Christians should remember they are the light and salt of the earth (Matthew 5). When the church fulfills its role as the light and salt, it will influence a world steeped in sin. Parents must be empowered to take their position and provide sex education to their children. As a pastor, licensed counselor, and sex therapist with three children, I felt the burden to put this book together to help you educate your children about the gift of sexuality. Here are a few things to know about this precious gift.

The Gift of Sex

Sex is a divine gift from our Creator, designed to offer a profound sense of physical, emotional, and spiritual intimacy that fosters unity between couples. However, in a fallen world, the concept of sex has been distorted to include both voluntary and involuntary intimate physical contact with areas of the body deemed sexual. This contact can involve oneself, a spouse, others, animals, or objects. Dr. Thomas explains that sex involves a level of stimulation, excitement, arousal, and/or orgasm in at least one of the individuals.

God's View of Sexuality

Our sexual conduct matters to God, and sex should be highly regarded and honored. Here are some key points:

Sexuality is God-Ordained and Blessed

- Genesis 1:27: "So God created man in his own image, in the image of God he created him; male and female he created them."

- Genesis 1:31: "God saw all that he had made, and it was very good. And there was evening, and there was morning—the sixth day."

- Marriage, partnership, and sexuality are inherently good and part of God's divine plan.

God's Regulations Concerning Sex

1. **Sexual Conduct Should Be in Sanctification and Honor**

   - God created sex and places limits on it. 1 Thessalonians 4:1-8: "It is God's will that you learn to possess your own body in sanctification and honor."

2. **Sex Should Be Honored and Kept Pure**

   - Hebrews 13:4 (The Message): "Honor marriage, and guard the sacredness of sexual intimacy between wife and husband. God draws a firm line against casual and illicit sex."

3. **Sexuality Should Not Be Abused**

   - Proverbs 5:1-23, especially 15-23, emphasizes the importance of keeping sexual relations within the boundaries of marriage, comparing it to the banks of a river that guide the water.

God's Guidelines on Sexual Conduct

1. **Moral Sex According to the Bible**

   - The Bible warns against using human passion or lust to define moral sex (Romans 1:24, 26; 13:13-14; 1 Thessalonians 4:5).

- Sexual activity conducted according to God's standards is enriching, fulfilling, and blessed.

2. **Sex within a Covenant Relationship**

- Sex is a means for married couples to open their relationship to the possibility of new life (procreation).

- Sex is not only permitted within marriage; it is essential for marital functioning (1 Corinthians 7:1-5).

3. **Premarital Sex Is Against God's Principles**

- Sex outside of a covenant relationship goes against God's intended purposes for this good but finite and now fallen gift.

- Non-marital sex is morally wrong because it does not fit with God's intended purposes.

Mental Integrity

- **God Requires Sexual Purity in Thought and Deed**

  - Sexual desire must be disciplined to be moral.

  - Inward sins of lust, such as thoughts of indulging in sexual sin, are wrong.

  - Stimulating lust through images of sexual sin is immoral at any age or under any circumstances.

- No sexual act can be moral if driven by desires that run contrary to the best interests of another person.

Dealing with Sexual Pleasure

1. **Stay Engaged with Your Purpose**

   - Focus on your goals and stay busy with activities that align with your values and purpose.

2. **Avoid Temptation in Advance**

   - Plan ahead to steer clear of situations that might lead to temptation.

3. **Discipline Your Mind**

   - Do not give Satan access to your thoughts. Be vigilant about what you allow into your mind.

4. **Manage Initial Cues**

   - It's not the first cue but the way it can trigger further sexual fantasies. Refuse to let these cues, like a bra strap or short shorts, lead your thoughts astray.

5. **Take Every Thought Captive**

   - 2 Corinthians 10:5: "We take captive every thought to make it obedient to Christ."

6. **Make a Covenant with Your Eyes**

    •   Follow Job's example in Job 31:1: "I made a covenant with my eyes not to look lustfully at a young woman."

POINTS TO REMEMBER:

Points To Know

Sexuality is a creation of God, intended to be celebrated within the sacred covenant relationship between a husband and a wife

Without proper guidance, teenagers are more prone to engaging in risky behaviors like unprotected sex or early sexual activity.

Chapter 2

Consequences of inadequate sex education from Home

Seeking Information from Reliable Sources

Sex education encompasses knowledge about body development, sexuality, and relationships, along with skill development, to empower young people in making informed decisions about their sexual health. When fathers are minimally involved in sexual and reproductive health (SRH) education, it can lead to several negative outcomes. Without paternal guidance, children may lack a comprehensive understanding of SRH, potentially resulting in misinformation and risky behaviors. Research indicates that adolescents who receive inadequate SRH education are more prone to engaging in high-risk sexual behaviors, experiencing unintended pregnancies, and contracting sexually transmitted infections (STIs)

Delaying the onset of sex education exacerbates these challenges, as adolescents may turn to peers and media for information, which can be inaccurate or harmful.

Here are several biblical perspectives on sex education:

- **Holistic Development:** Sex education in its broadest sense promotes the fullest development of individuals as male and female, embracing their God-given qualities.

- **Character Development:** It involves character education, recognizing that sex differentiation encompasses more than just anatomy but also individual temperaments.

- **Gift of God:** Sex education emphasizes viewing sexuality as a gift from God and understanding how to honor it for His glory.

When parents do not effectively communicate about sex, their children may seek information from unreliable sources such as peers or the internet. This can perpetuate myths and misconceptions, like the false belief that one cannot contract an STD from oral sex, leading to risky behaviors driven by ignorance of potential consequences.

Addressing Peer Influence in Sex Education

Delaying sex education can have profound effects on adolescents, as they may already be influenced by peers who provide incomplete or misleading information.

Impact of Peer Influence on Risky Behaviors

Peers can significantly influence attitudes and behaviors related to sex, often promoting risky actions and perpetuating myths that can lead to premature sexual experiences. For instance, young people might hear from friends that engaging in sexual activity is a rite of passage or that it will enhance their social status.

Without the guidance of trusted adults, children may feel pressured to conform to these peer norms, increasing the likelihood of engaging in risky sexual behaviors without fully understanding the potential consequences.

The Crucial Timing of Sex Education

Experts emphasize the importance of initiating sex education early and utilizing "teachable moments" throughout a child's development (DeFreitas, 1998; Gordon & Gordon, 2000; Planned Parenthood, 1996; Woody, 2002). These proactive discussions help children form a healthy understanding of sex and relationships before external influences take hold.

Unfortunately, many parents still view sex education as a singular conversation reserved for adolescence. This outdated approach misses opportunities to establish a solid foundation of knowledge and values that can support adolescents as they navigate their formative years.

Adolescents Feeling Unprepared to Make Informed Decisions

Delayed sex education can leave adolescents feeling ill-prepared to make informed decisions regarding their sexual health. Without proper guidance, teenagers are more prone to engaging in risky behaviors like unprotected sex or early sexual activity. These decisions can have lasting repercussions, such as increased rates of sexually transmitted infections (STIs) and unintended pregnancies. Research indicates that comprehensive sex education, starting early and including open discussions about all aspects of sexuality, can significantly mitigate these risks.

Peer Influence on Boys' Sexual Education

Peers exert a significant influence on the sexual education of adolescent boys. Boys often cite friends as their primary and most frequent sources of sexual information. Although specific studies documenting the values and messages conveyed by peers are limited, existing research suggests that peer discussions cover various topics, including sexual intercourse, HIV/AIDS, contraception, romantic relationships, and pregnancy. The impact of peer pressure on boys' sexual behaviors can be profound. Pressure from peers can lead boys to engage in sexual activities earlier than they might otherwise choose, often to prove their masculinity or fit in, sometimes without adequate knowledge or preparation.

Media as a Dominant Source of Sexual Information

The media serves as another primary source of sexual education for boys. Surveys indicate that a significant proportion of young men acquire information about sex from media sources, which include discussions about AIDS, STDs, and condom use. Media content frequently incorporates sexual imagery and messages that shape young men's perceptions and expectations about sexual experiences.

However, media portrayals of sex can be misleading and contribute to unrealistic expectations. Television shows, movies, and music videos often depict sex as glamorous and devoid of consequences, neglecting the complexities and responsibilities involved. This skewed representation can foster misunderstandings and promote unhealthy attitudes towards sexual relationships.

Shyness and Shame

Moreover, insufficient communication exacerbates a culture of secrecy and shame surrounding sexuality, making it challenging for boys to seek assistance or guidance when facing issues or uncertainties. This reluctance can result in enduring challenges concerning sexual health and relationships. For instance, a boy feeling ashamed or uncomfortable discussing sex may avoid seeking medical care for symptoms of an STD, allowing the condition to escalate and potentially leading to serious health consequences.

Low Self-Esteem

On a psychological level, inadequate communication about sex can negatively impact boys' self-esteem and body image. Without constructive guidance, they might develop unrealistic expectations about sex and relationships based on media portrayals, which can lead to dissatisfaction and confusion. This, in turn, can strain their emotional well-being and interpersonal connections.

In cultures where discussions about sexuality and sexual health are taboo, many girls and young women encounter profound shocks upon reaching puberty. For example, studies reveal that in various cultural contexts, refugee women often report having no prior knowledge about menstruation before experiencing menarche. Similarly, many women had little understanding of pregnancy until they became pregnant with their first child. Consequently, this lack of information contributes to significant health issues. Some women describe their first menstruation as a painful and secretive experience, coupled with feelings of anxiety and shock on their wedding nights.

Chapter 3

―――――∧―――――

Why start early

Pre-Adolescence: A Critical and Curious Period

Pre-adolescence is a critical period marked by curiosity and susceptibility to temptation. According to Guilamo-Ramos and his research team, this stage is the most appropriate time for parents to begin conversations about sexual health with their children, as they have not yet become sexually active.

The timing of sex education is crucial. Experts recommend that parents start these conversations early and take advantage of "teachable moments" as they arise in the child's life, regardless of age. Early and ongoing discussions can help children develop a healthy understanding of sex and relationships before they are influenced by external factors. However, many parents still view sex education as a one-time talk that should occur only when their children reach adolescence. This outdated approach often leads to missed opportunities to establish a solid foundation of knowledge and values to guide adolescents through their formative years.

1. It is during early to middle adolescence (ages 10–17) that most individuals become aware of their sexuality, experience sexual thoughts, and engage in sexual activity.

2. In all cultures, the preadolescent years are a critical period for addressing sexual health issues. Adolescents face particular health risks and need education on sexual health.

3. Child development from early to middle adolescence is a crucial period for parental discussions about sexuality. Often, the responsibility of sexual health and sex education falls on public school educators. In the United States, teachers who provide sexuality education frequently encounter conflicts with immigrant families whose views on sex education differ.

4. As children develop into adolescents, new challenges arise between them and their parents.

5. Preadolescents account for 23% of the overall burden of disease (disability-adjusted life years) due to pregnancy and childbirth (Patton et al., 2009). Annually, 16 million births occur to young

women aged 15–19 years, representing 11% of all births (Sawyer et al., 2012).

6. Approximately 2.5 million births occur to girls aged 12–15 years in low-resource countries each year, with around a million births to girls younger than 16 years in Africa (Neal et al., 2012).

7. Moreover, early childbearing is linked with higher maternal mortality and morbidity rates, and an increased risk of induced (mostly illegal and unsafe) abortions.

8. Complications related to childbearing and maternal health issues are the leading cause of death among adolescent females.

9. Shame may also influence how adolescents communicate sexual health concerns. Children who have experienced sexual trauma may struggle to talk about their ordeal. Traumatized children often feel powerless to open up and discuss their experiences.

Sex Education from School is not enough

Although many public school systems offer programs introducing sexual health and sexuality, students often lack crucial guidance and support from their parents. Parent communication is essential for reinforcing the information presented in schools. However, many parents from diverse backgrounds face challenges in initiating conversations about sexuality. Culture and ethnicity are important factors to consider when examining why some parents struggle with these discussions.

a. Puberty years are critical and require parents to provide support and meaningful education. Curiosity and experimentation are common during adolescent psychosexual development.

b. In all cultures, the preadolescent years are a crucial period for addressing sexual health issues.

c. In cultures where conversations about sexuality and sexual health are forbidden, many girls and young women face shock when they reach puberty.

d. Adolescents who experience healthy relationships are more likely to have healthy relationships in young adulthood.

e. A lack of knowledge and information can lead to health issues. Some women describe their menarche as a painful experience, involving concealed bleeding and feelings of anxiety on wedding nights.

Sex Education: An Essential Component of Adolescent Development

Sex education encompasses the provision of knowledge about body development, sex, sexuality, and relationships, along with the development of skills to help young people communicate about sex and make informed decisions about their sexual health.

Without parental guidance, children may lack a comprehensive understanding of sexual and reproductive health (SRH), leading to misinformation and risky behaviors. Studies have shown that adolescents who do not receive adequate SRH education are more likely to engage in high-risk sexual behaviors, experience unintended pregnancies, and contract sexually transmitted infections (STIs) (Kirby, 2007). Starting sex education too late exacerbates these issues, as adolescents are more likely to turn to peers and the media for information, which can be inaccurate or harmful.

When parents fail to communicate effectively about sex, their children may seek information from unreliable sources such as peers or the internet. This can lead to the dissemination of myths and misconceptions about sex and sexual health. For example, a common myth is that one cannot contract an STD from oral sex, which is false and can result in individuals engaging in risky behavior without understanding the potential consequences.

Competing with Peers: The Impact of Delayed Sex Education

Starting sex education too late can have significant consequences for adolescents. By the time many parents initiate these conversations, their children may already be influenced by their peers, who can provide misleading or incomplete information.

Influence of Peers on Risky Behaviors

Peers often promote risky behaviors or perpetuate myths about sex that can lead to unsafe practices. For example, a teenager who learns about sex primarily from friends might believe that they are not cool if they do not practice sexual behaviors

The Importance of Timing in Sex Education

The timing of sex education is crucial. Experts recommend that parents start these conversations early and take advantage of "teachable moments" as they arise in the child's life, regardless of age. Early and ongoing discussions can help children develop a healthy understanding of sex and relationships before they are exposed to external influences. However, many parents still view sex education as a one-time talk that should occur only when their children reach adolescence. This outdated notion often results in missed opportunities to build a foundation of knowledge and values that can guide adolescents through their formative years.

POINTS TO KNOW

Without proper guidance, teenagers are more prone to engaging in risky behaviors like unprotected sex or early sexual activity.

Chapter 4

———∧———

The importance of parent-child sexual health and relationship education

Here we go, let's start with:

Sexuality and Early Curiosity

Sexuality is one of the many questions toddlers have. They want to know where they come from and understand what they experience and feel. Discussing sexuality should be an integral part of their education. Talking about sexuality throughout their development provides essential keys to a healthy sex life. According to a study by Planned Parenthood, friends are the first people young people turn to when discussing sexuality. However, more than half of the young people surveyed believe that parents have the greatest responsibility in this area.

Research shows that adolescents who are in healthy relationships are more likely to:

- Feel better about themselves

- Have higher self-esteem

- Achieve more in school

- Have better relationships with their families

The Importance of Early Conversations about Sexuality

Children's exposure to information about sexuality begins much earlier than many parents realize. If parents do not discuss sexuality with their children, they lose control over what and how they learn about it. Without parental guidance, children will learn about sexuality from other sources, such as friends or the internet. Jean Kilbourne, a specialist in the image of women in advertising, emphasizes that "sex is trivialized in pornography, the media, and advertising like nowhere else." The distorted and unrealistic visions of sexual relations presented in these mediums shape young people's expectations and can distort their understanding of normal relationships.

The Serious Ramifications of a Lack of Sexual Health Education

The lack of comprehensive sexual health education can have serious consequences. A poor understanding of sex can lead to discomfort or avoidance of the topic altogether. However, sexual health education is broad and essential. It includes knowledge about bodily development, sex, sexuality, and relationships, along with skills-building to help young people make informed decisions regarding their sexual health. Providing this education helps ensure that young people develop a healthy, realistic understanding of sexuality and relationships.

Equipping young people with the skills and tools to make healthy decisions about sex and relationships is far more effective than denying them information and simply telling them not to engage in sexual activity.

Most sex education provided by parents primarily comes from mothers, and these discussions often focus on basic facts or warnings rather than offering comprehensive guidance. Young people need sexual health and relationship education to avoid the dangers present in society today. Without relationship skills, teenagers struggle to navigate the complexities of dating.

To prepare for the future, individuals need to:

- Understand self-concept

- Increase their knowledge and understanding of relationships, sex, and sexual health

- Gain the confidence and ability to practice safety in all aspects of sexual relationships

- Know about and feel comfortable accessing a range of services and people for support

- Develop skills to establish and maintain respectful and positive relationships

- Foster positive attitudes and behaviors related to sexual health and relationships, including an appreciation for sexual, cultural, and physical diversity

Adolescents Feel Unprepared

Limited engagement from parents leaves many adolescents feeling unprepared and unsupported as they navigate their sexual development. In 2000, an American study entitled "Adolescent Sexuality and the Media" showed that teenagers witnessed nearly 150 explicit sexual scenes on television per week. Often, the small screen does not reflect safe and healthy intimate relationships. These portrayals tend to glamorize, degrade, and exploit sexuality, promoting promiscuity, the objectification of women, and aggressive attitudes as normal elements of intimate relationships. This distorted portrayal can negatively impact young people's self-esteem and behavior, leading to confusion about what constitutes a respectful and consensual relationship.

Given this landscape, it's crucial for parents to actively engage in protecting their children online.

Having conversations about sexual health with your child is important. Regardless of the subject, these discussions strengthen the relationship of trust and divert attention away from peers or the internet. A child or teenager who trusts their parent is less likely to withdraw and more likely to talk about their doubts and concerns. The role of the parent is to support their child and teach them to become independent.

Here are 12 topics you can teach your teenagers as you prepare them for marriage:

1. The importance of mutual respect in relationships.

2. Understanding consent and boundaries.

3. Recognizing healthy vs. unhealthy relationships.

4. Effective communication skills.

5. Managing peer pressure.

6. The realities of sexual media portrayals.

7. Basic knowledge of reproductive health.

8. The significance of emotional intimacy.

9. Safe sex practices and contraception.

10. Navigating digital relationships and privacy.

11. The impact of pornography on perceptions of sex.

12. Building self-esteem and body positivity.

POINTS TO REMEMBER

Talking about sexuality throughout their development provides

essential keys to a healthy sex life.

Chapter 5

Youth challenges in discussing sexuality and relationships with parents

Sexuality Education: What Does This Imply?

The challenges youths face in discussing sexuality and relationships with their parents are multifaceted and deeply rooted in cultural, emotional, and communicative barriers. Addressing these challenges requires a concerted effort from parents, educators, and the broader community to create an environment where open and informed discussions about sexual health and well-being can thrive. Through these efforts, we can bridge the communication gap and ensure that adolescents receive the comprehensive sex education they need to make informed and responsible decisions about their sexual health.

In the United States, the Sexuality Information and Education Council of the United States (SIECUS) defines sexuality education as "a lifelong process of acquiring information and forming attitudes, beliefs, and values about identity, relationships, and intimacy." SIECUS suggests that sexuality education should address a wide range of issues, including personality, values, decision-making, peer and social pressures, intimacy, affection, body image, gender roles, communication strategies, and various sexual behaviors (SIECUS, 2008).

Sexuality Education in Australia

In Australia, sexuality education has been described as an integral part of life that influences personality, beginning at birth and continuing until death. Significant life events highlight aspects of sexuality, such as puberty, menopause, choosing a partner, and childbirth. Sexuality is culturally defined and influenced by factors including family, peers, religion, economics, school, media, law, and science.

These definitions indicate that sexuality education is not confined to the home, school, or formal settings but is a continuous part of life. The term 'sexuality education' signifies a comprehensive approach to helping young people develop competence and confidence as they navigate their sexual lives, aiming to prevent issues such as unintended pregnancies and the spread of sexually transmitted infections.

Research highlights that while youths express a desire to engage in these conversations with their parents, various emotional and social barriers often impede these discussions. This article explores these challenges, focusing on the discomfort, embarrassment, and gender dynamics that affect communication between parents and their teenage or young adult children about sexual matters.

Desire for Parental Communication

Discussing sexuality and relationships with parents is a vital aspect of comprehensive sex education, yet it presents significant challenges for many young people. Research indicates that young people generally want to discuss these topics with their parents, particularly with their mothers. This preference is rooted in the perception that mothers are more approachable and understanding when it comes to sensitive topics.

According to a study by Smith, Agius, Dyson, Mitchell, and Pitts (2003), high levels of discomfort and embarrassment are commonly associated with these conversations, significantly deterring open dialogue between parents and their children. Many adolescents report feeling awkward and uneasy when trying to initiate conversations about sexuality and relationships with their parents. This discomfort often stems from the fear of judgment or misunderstanding. For instance, one participant in the study mentioned that although they wanted to talk to their mother about dating and sexual health, they were apprehensive about her reaction, worrying that she might either overreact or dismiss their concerns.

Interestingly, the study found that when parents, particularly mothers, are proactive in initiating these discussions and approach the topic with openness and empathy, it can significantly reduce the discomfort felt by their children. Adolescents reported feeling more at ease and more likely to engage in meaningful conversations when they sensed that their parents were knowledgeable and non-judgmental.

Let me share you a story of my cousin, I will call her Emily, Emily is a 15-year-old girl who had been dating her boyfriend, Jake, for a few months and had many questions about relationships and sexual health. She really wanted to talk to her mother, Susan, about these topics because she trusted her and valued her advice. However, Emily felt extremely nervous about initiating the conversation. She worried that her mother might overreact; lecturing her about the dangers of teenage relationships instead of providing the guidance she sought. One evening, as they were preparing dinner together, Emily mustered up the courage to bring up the topic. "Mom," she began hesitantly, "can I ask you something about relationships?"

Susan sensed her daughter's unease and decided to create a safe and open environment for the discussion. She put down the knife she was using to chop vegetables and turned to face Emily, giving her full attention. "Of course, sweetheart," she said gently. "You can ask me anything." Encouraged by her mother's calm demeanor, Emily continued, "Well, I've been thinking a lot about my relationship with Jake, and I have some questions about, you know, sex and how to make sure we're both being safe and respectful."

Susan took a deep breath, recalling her own awkward teenage years. She understood the importance of being supportive and informative without showing judgment or discomfort in this moment. "I'm really glad you're thinking about these things, Emily," she said warmly. "It's completely normal to have questions. Let's talk about what's on your mind, and I'll do my best to help."

Over the next hour, they discussed various aspects of relationships, including emotional readiness, consent, and safe sex practices. Susan listened carefully to Emily's concerns and answered her questions honestly. She shared her own experiences and values, ensuring the conversation remained balanced and non-judgmental.

By the end of their talk, Emily felt a tremendous sense of relief. She was grateful to have her mother to turn to for advice and felt more confident about navigating her relationship with Jake. Susan, in turn, was glad she had handled the conversation well, reinforcing their bond and ensuring that Emily felt supported.

This story illustrates how, despite initial discomfort, an open and empathetic approach from parents can facilitate meaningful and informative discussions about sexuality and relationships. When parents like Susan create a safe space for dialogue, it helps young people like Emily feel understood and better prepared to make informed decisions.

What Adolescents Hear and What They Really Want to Hear

Research indicates that young people generally desire to discuss sexuality and relationships with their parents, especially their mothers. This preference is based on the perception that mothers are more approachable and understanding regarding sensitive topics. Researchers highlights that high levels of discomfort and embarrassment are commonly associated with these conversations, significantly deterring open dialogue between parents and their children. However, there are challenges to these discussions.

Adolescents Often Hear Warnings

When parents attempt to communicate about sexual health, adolescents frequently hear warnings, prohibitions, and fear-based messages. Statements such as "Don't have sex until you're older," "You should avoid having close contact with men," or "Avoid these behaviors" are often perceived as authoritarian and dismissive of their experiences and feelings. These messages can lead to resistance, confusion, or a sense of being misunderstood.

Instead of feeling informed and prepared, adolescents often hear conversations emphasizing the risks and negative consequences of sexual activity without sufficient guidance on managing their sexual health responsibly. This approach can leave them feeling scared or confused rather than empowered and knowledgeable.

Many adolescents report feeling awkward and uneasy when trying to initiate conversations about sexuality and relationships with their parents. This discomfort often arises from the fear of being judged or misunderstood by their parents. For instance, one study participant mentioned that although they wanted to talk to their mother about dating and sexual health, they were apprehensive about her reaction, worrying that she might either overreact or dismiss their concerns.

Teenagers also express frustration with the preachy tone many parents adopt during these conversations. Instead of engaging in a two-way dialogue where teenagers can ask questions and express their feelings, parents often lecture about the dangers of sex or insist on abstinence without addressing the broader aspects of sexual health and relationships. This approach not only fails to provide the necessary information but also alienates teenagers, making them less likely to turn to their parents for advice and support in the future.

Moreover, when parents do attempt to talk to their children about sex, these conversations are often quite limited and superficial. Most sex education provided by parents comes primarily from mothers, and even then, the discussions are often restricted to basic facts or warnings rather than comprehensive guidance.

The Feeling of Unpreparedness

This limited engagement leaves many adolescents feeling unprepared and unsupported as they navigate their sexual development. Consequently, most teenagers report learning very little about sex from their parents and are often unaware of their parents' values regarding sexual behavior. They frequently complain that parents do not engage in meaningful discussions but instead tend to preach, simply telling them not to have sex and assuming that any youth who asks about sex must already be sexually active. As a result, many adolescents feel ill-equipped to handle their sexual development and make informed decisions.

Emotional Barriers: Discomfort and Embarrassment

Embarrassment constitutes a primary reason young people avoid discussing sexual matters with their parents. According to Smith et al. (2003), many teenagers and young adults feel highly uncomfortable and embarrassed when talking about sex with their parents. This discomfort can stem from several sources:

- **Personal Shyness:** Many young people report feeling too shy to bring up the topic of sex with their parents. This shyness often relates to the intimate nature of the subject and the fear of being judged or misunderstood.

- **Perception of Privacy:** Some students believe that discussions about sex are too personal to share with family members. They may feel that these topics should be kept private and not discussed openly within the family environment.

- **Lack of Immediate Need:** Others indicate that they do not feel the need to discuss sex and relationships with their parents because they do not currently face any related issues or questions. This lack of perceived necessity can delay important conversations until it might be too late to provide useful guidance.

Gender Dynamics in Communication

Gender dynamics significantly influence how youths communicate with their parents about sexuality and relationships. Studies have shown a marked preference among young people to discuss these topics with their mothers rather than their fathers. This preference is due to several factors:

- **Approachability of Mothers:** Mothers are generally seen as more approachable and empathetic, making them the preferred parent for these sensitive discussions. This perception is reinforced by traditional gender roles that often cast mothers as the primary caregivers and emotional support figures within the family.

- **Distant Relationships with Fathers:** Boys, in particular, tend to distance themselves from their mothers during puberty and may not feel comfortable discussing sexual matters with their fathers due to a lack of close, communicative relationships. Fathers may also avoid these discussions due to their own discomfort or lack of preparedness, leaving a gap in support for their sons.

- **Bias and Misconceptions:** Girls might find it easier to talk to their mothers, but these conversations can also be fraught with challenges. Mothers might project their own anxieties and misconceptions about sex onto their daughters, leading to incomplete or biased information being shared.

Impact of Inadequate Communication

The lack of open communication about sex and relationships between parents and their children can have significant consequences. Young people who do not receive comprehensive sex education at home are at greater risk of engaging in unsafe sexual behaviors. Studies have shown that youths whose parents discuss sexual health and safe sex practices with them are more likely to delay sexual initiation and use contraception when they become sexually active.

POINTS TO REMEMBER

Research indicates that young people generally desire to discuss sexuality and relationships with their parents, especially their mothers

Chapter 6

Young Boys
Receive Little Sex Education

B oys often receive inadequate sex education compared to girls, which can have significant implications for their sexual health and behavior. Parents, peers, and media influence how boys perceive sex, but these sources often provide incomplete or misleading information. Addressing cultural and societal barriers and encouraging parental involvement can create an environment where boys feel comfortable seeking accurate information and guidance. This approach aims to foster healthier and more respectful attitudes towards sexuality.

Sex education is crucial for adolescent development, equipping them with the knowledge to make informed decisions about sexual health. However, there remains a noticeable disparity between how boys and girls receive this education. While efforts have prioritized educating girls on issues like pregnancy prevention and consent, boys frequently lack sufficient guidance on these critical topics.

In many African-American communities, there's a distinct pattern in how parents advise their children before they leave home for school or move to new cities. Advice given to sons often emphasizes self-awareness and avoiding negative influences upon arrival, while daughters typically receive more protective and detailed guidance, emphasizing safety and caution in relationships and social interactions. These differences reflect broader societal norms and expectations regarding gender and sexual health education.

Closing this educational gap is essential to ensuring that all young people, regardless of gender, receive comprehensive sexual health education. This article explores where boys learn about sex, the content of these sources, and the implications of this knowledge gap.

The Role of Parents in Sex Education

Parents have traditionally been seen as primary sources of sexual information for their children. However, studies indicate that many adolescent boys report receiving little to no communication about sex from their parents. When parents do discuss sex, the conversation often revolves around topics like safety and contraception. Subjects such as sexual pleasure—including masturbation, orgasms, and wet dreams—are frequently neglected. This limited scope prevents boys from gaining a thorough understanding of sexuality, leading them to rely more on peers and media for information.

For example, a study involving 286 male undergraduates revealed that boys received significantly less sexual communication from their parents compared to their peers and media sources (Kaiser Family Foundation, 2005). When parents do engage in conversations about sex, the focus tends to be on abstinence and contraception, whereas messages from peers and media often promote more positive views on sex.

Peer Influence on Sexual Education

Peers play a significant role in the sexual education of adolescent boys. Boys often cite peers and friends as their most frequent and important sources of sexual information (Ballard & Morris, 1998). Although research on the specific values and messages communicated by peers is limited, available studies suggest that peer communication covers a range of issues, including sexual intercourse, HIV/AIDS, contraception, romantic relationships, and pregnancy. The influence of peers on boys' sexual behaviors can be profound. Peer pressure often encourages boys to engage in sexual activities earlier than they might otherwise choose, leading to risky behaviors. For example, boys may feel compelled to prove their masculinity by boasting about sexual conquests or engaging in sexual activities without adequate knowledge or preparation.

Media as a Dominant Source of Sexual Information

The media is another dominant source of sexual education for boys. Surveys indicate that a high percentage of young men report gaining information about sex from the media, including information on AIDS, STDs, and condoms. Media content frequently includes sexual imagery and messages, shaping young men's perceptions and expectations about sex. However, media portrayals of sex can be misleading and contribute to unrealistic expectations. Television shows, movies, and music videos often depict sex as glamorous and consequence-free, without addressing the complexities and responsibilities involved. This skewed portrayal can lead to misunderstandings and unhealthy attitudes towards sex.

High-Risk Sexual Behaviors

Limited parental communication about sex can have several negative consequences. Boys who lack accurate and comprehensive information are more likely to engage in risky sexual behaviors. Additionally, they may develop unhealthy attitudes towards sex, viewing it solely as a physical act rather than an aspect of a healthy, respectful relationship.

When parents fail to communicate effectively about sex, their children may seek information from unreliable sources such as peers or the internet. This can lead to the dissemination of myths and misconceptions about sex and sexual health. For example, a common myth is that one cannot contract an STD from oral sex, which is false and can result in individuals engaging in risky behavior without understanding the potential consequences.

Difficulty Seeking Help Due to Sexual Silence and Shame

The lack of open communication can perpetuate a culture of silence and shame around sex, making it difficult for boys to seek help or advice when they encounter problems or have questions. This can lead to long-term issues with sexual health and relationships. For instance, a boy who feels ashamed or uncomfortable discussing sex might not seek medical attention for symptoms of an STD, allowing the infection to worsen and potentially causing serious health problems.

Self-Esteem Issues

Psychologically, inadequate communication about sex can negatively impact boys' self-esteem and body image. Without positive guidance, they may develop unrealistic expectations about sex and relationships based on media portrayals, leading to dissatisfaction and confusion. This can further strain their emotional well-being and interpersonal relationships.

Conversely, open and honest communication about sex can have positive effects. Boys who receive accurate information from their parents are more likely to delay sexual activity and use contraception when they do become sexually active. This not only reduces the risk of STDs and unintended pregnancies but also promotes healthier attitudes toward sex and relationships. For example, sex education that includes discussions about consent, healthy relationships, and sexual pleasure is essential for boys. Such education can help boys develop a balanced and respectful understanding of sexuality, reducing the likelihood of risky behaviors and promoting healthy relationships.

Addressing Cultural and Societal Barriers

Cultural and societal barriers often impede open discussions about sex. In many cultures, talking about sex is considered taboo, which prevents boys from seeking information and guidance. Addressing these barriers requires a multi-faceted approach that includes educating parents, creating supportive community environments, and advocating for policy changes.

Encouraging Parental Involvement

Parents need encouragement and resources to effectively talk to their sons about sex. Educational programs for parents can provide the knowledge and skills necessary for open and honest discussions with their children. Workshops and resources offering tips on approaching sensitive topics can empower parents to become effective communicators about sexual health.

POINTS TO REMEMBER

Limited parental communication about sex can have several negative consequences. Boys who lack accurate and comprehensive information are more likely to engage in risky sexual behaviors.

Chapter 7

Parents are the best source

Parents and caregivers serve as the foundation for children's sexual development

Many people think that parent-child sexual talks only involve discussions about safe sex and contraception, such as using condoms to prevent pregnancies. However, these conversations encompass a wide range of topics related to sexual health, relationships, and behavior. The goal is to equip young people with the knowledge, values, and skills they need to make informed and responsible decisions about their sexual health.

Research consistently shows that parent-child communication about sex-related topics during adolescence can significantly reduce risky sexual behaviors, such as exposure to pornography, and sexually transmitted diseases (STDs). Effective communication can also promote sexual boundaries and decrease the likelihood of unwanted pregnancies. Therefore, such discussions are a crucial element in every family.

Often, family members feel isolated because they build walls of separation rather than bridges of communication and love. They spend more time on media, television, radio, and the internet than with each other. Effective communication is essential for understanding one another, expressing thoughts, offering comfort, learning, and many other benefits.

Communication involves participating in another person's life and sharing the best parts of yourself. The true motive for communication should be the desire to give others the most valuable things you have.

Research has shown that parents can predict individual attitudes and sexual risk-taking during parent-child communication. This ability helps parents understand their child's perspectives and guide them more effectively. Studies indicate that open and honest discussions about sexual health and attitudes can lead to more informed and cautious decisions by adolescents.

By recognizing the nuances in their children's responses and attitudes, parents can tailor their guidance to address specific concerns and misconceptions, fostering a healthier and more responsible approach to sexual behavior.

Reducing Sexual Risk during Adolescence

Understanding parent-child communication about sex is crucial, given that adolescents face a high risk of adverse sexual health outcomes. The United States has the highest rate of teenage pregnancies among developed nations, with adolescents accounting for nearly half of all new STI cases each year (Centers for Disease Control and Prevention, 2013). Sexual risk during adolescence remains a significant issue in the twenty-first century. Reducing teenage pregnancies and STIs and increasing the number of early adolescents (ages 10-16) who practice sexual abstinence are primary health goals for parents, educators, and health professionals.

Sexual risk-taking during adolescence includes behaviors such as early sexual initiation, having multiple sexual partners, and inconsistent or non-use of contraception. These behaviors increase the likelihood of negative outcomes such as sexually transmitted infections (STIs) and unintended pregnancies. Effective parent-child communication about sexual health can play a crucial role in mitigating these risks. When parents proactively discuss these topics, they can help their children understand the consequences of risky sexual behavior and encourage safer practices.

Parents as Primary Sexual Socializing Agents

Parents are the primary sexual socializing agents for their children, whose supervision significantly impacts their sexual attitudes. They convey attitudes, values, and norms through frequent and open communication. Research by Jaccard and Dittus (2000) and Whitaker and Miller (2000) underscore the importance of ongoing dialogue between parents and adolescents about sexual behavior. In studies of rural African American youth, Murry et al. (2005) found that regular parent-child discussions about risk behaviors, including sexuality, enable parents to set clear expectations and effectively transmit their norms.

Martino and his research team also highlight those ongoing conversations, rather than a single "big talk," are more effective in reinforcing values and expectations. Repeated dialogues allow the conversation to evolve naturally as the adolescent matures and their understanding deepens. This continuous engagement helps maintain an open line of communication, ensuring that adolescents feel comfortable seeking guidance as needed.

Below are some of the benefits of parent-child sex education:

- **Setting Clear Expectations:** Regular discussions enable parents to convey their expectations regarding sexual behavior effectively.

- **Reinforcing Values:** Continuous conversations help reinforce family values and norms.

- **Comfort and Openness:** Maintaining an open line of communication ensures that adolescents feel comfortable seeking guidance.

- **Risk Reduction:** Effective communication can mitigate risky behaviors by providing accurate information and promoting safer practices.

- **Enhanced Understanding:** As adolescents mature, ongoing dialogues allow for a deeper understanding of sexual health and relationships.

Increasing Understanding of Sexual Relationship Development

Warm and responsive parenting practices profoundly impact children's sexual health outcomes. By fostering open communication, providing emotional support, setting clear expectations, and modeling healthy relationships, parents can guide their children toward making informed and responsible sexual choices. Research highlights the importance of these practices, emphasizing the need for parents to actively engage in their children's lives and support their development in all aspects, including sexual health.

Making Informed Decisions

While open communication is essential, setting clear expectations and boundaries is equally crucial. Parents should articulate their values and expectations regarding sexual behavior, explaining the reasons behind these guidelines. This clarity helps children understand the importance of making responsible choices.

Parenting practices play a pivotal role in shaping children's behavior, values, and overall development. Warm and responsive parenting has been shown to have significant positive effects on children's sexual health outcomes. For instance, adolescents who experience warm and responsive parenting are more likely to delay the onset of sexual activity. Additionally, open and supportive communication about sexual health between parents and children fosters a sense of trust, making it easier for children to seek guidance and make informed decisions about their sexual behaviors.

Helping Young People Overcome Peer Pressure

Some young people struggle to resist unwanted sex or feel pressured to exchange sex for money. Comprehensive sexuality education (CSE) can help them understand concepts such as consent, acceptance, and tolerance, as well as the serious consequences of rape.

Positive, supportive conversations between parents and their children are instrumental in fostering self-pride and a healthy self-image. Crosby et al. (2003) found that such interactions buffer youths against negative peer influences and shape their perceptions of sexually active peers. When adolescents have a strong sense of self-worth, they are less likely to succumb to peer pressure and engage in risky sexual behaviors. Furthermore, these meaningful dialogues can establish trust, making children feel more comfortable seeking advice from their parents rather than relying on potentially misleading information from peers.

Developing Positive Attitudes and Beliefs on Sexuality

Children's beliefs about sexuality are significantly influenced by their parents' supervision and monitoring. When parents create a nurturing environment where children feel valued and heard, children are more likely to adopt their parents' attitudes towards sex, which typically emphasize caution and responsibility. A warm and responsive relationship increases the likelihood that children will internalize their parents' expectations and values, reducing their dependence on peer value systems and leading to healthier sexual behaviors.

Clear Expectations and Values

Parents act as key socializing agents, conveying attitudes, values, and norms to their children. More studies underscores the importance of frequent and open communication between parents and adolescents about sexual behavior. Studies of rural African American youth by Murry et al. (2005) found that regular parent-child discussions about risk behaviors, including sexuality, enable parents to set clear expectations and effectively transmit their norms. Contrary to popular belief, sexuality education does not increase the incidence of sexual activity, sexual risk-taking behavior, or STI/HIV infection rates among young people.

Emotional Support and Sexual Health

Emotional support is fundamental in fostering healthy sexual behaviors. Parents should reassure their children that they can approach them with any concerns or questions without fear of criticism. This support builds trust and encourages ongoing dialogue. The emotional and instrumental support provided during these conversations is crucial. Adolescents who perceive their parents as supportive and non-judgmental are more likely to engage in open discussions about sexuality. Brody et al. (1998) highlighted that youths who feel their parents will listen without criticism are more inclined to seek their guidance on sexual matters.

For instance, consider a scenario where a father notices his teenage daughter feeling anxious about attending a school dance. Instead of imposing strict rules or showing disapproval, he sits down with her, shares stories from his own adolescence, and discusses the importance of making safe choices. This supportive approach not only eases her anxiety but also instills confidence in her to make responsible decisions.

Additionally, the consistency and frequency of these discussions are important. A study by Martino et al. (2008) emphasize that ongoing conversations, rather than a single "big talk," are more effective in reinforcing values and expectations. Repeated dialogues allow for the natural evolution of the conversation as the adolescent matures and their understanding deepens. This continuous engagement helps maintain an open line of communication, ensuring that adolescents feel comfortable seeking guidance as needed.

The Challenges of the Parent-Child "Sex Talk"

Discomfort

The "sex talk" between parents and children is fraught with challenges. Many parents feel uncomfortable or unprepared to discuss sexual topics, often due to their own upbringing or cultural taboos surrounding the subject. This discomfort can lead to avoidance or incomplete conversations, leaving adolescents without the comprehensive information they need.

Myth that Children Will Act Out

Additionally, parents might fear that talking about sex will encourage sexual activity, despite evidence suggesting that open communication can actually delay sexual initiation and promote safer behaviors. Adolescents, on the other hand, may feel embarrassed or defensive during these discussions, perceiving them as intrusive or patronizing.

They might also worry about disappointing their parents or fear judgment, which can hinder open and honest dialogue.

Overcoming Barriers

Effective communication requires overcoming these emotional barriers and establishing a trusting, respectful environment where adolescents feel safe to express their thoughts and questions without fear of reprimand. To address these challenges, parents can use strategies for discussing sexual health in a more comfortable and effective manner. This includes understanding the developmental stages of adolescents, employing age-appropriate language, and creating an ongoing dialogue rather than a one-time conversation.

Supportive Approach

By approaching the topic with empathy, openness, and accurate information, parents can better support their children in making informed and responsible decisions about their sexual health. Parenting practices play a pivotal role in shaping children's behavior, values, and overall development. Among these practices, warm and responsive parenting has been shown to have significant positive effects on children's sexual health outcomes.

The Authoritative Parent

The authoritative parenting style is characterized by parents who rationalize directives to their children, explaining the reasons behind demands, disciplines, policies, and values in a nonjudgmental atmosphere. Authoritative parents allow room for mistakes but use power when necessary and maintain control while setting rules for their child's development. This style produces positive outcomes in a child's development (Baumrind, 1991) and generates warmth and affection, differing significantly from the authoritarian parenting style.

The Authoritarian Parent

The authoritarian parenting style values and focuses on obedience, often preferring punitive measures for discipline. Authoritarian parents exercise control in a way that restricts the child's autonomy, driven by the belief that children are self-willed and strong and therefore need their will to be bent through authority figures such as the church, school, and parents.

Studies have shown that the authoritarian style tends to be one-sided, with communication flowing from parent to child. While parents have high expectations and children may be obedient, the children's self-esteem and moral reasoning (values and ideas about sexuality) are often lower. Authoritarian parents rarely engage in dialogues with their children; instead, they talk at them.

The Permissive Parent

Permissive parents exhibit characteristics of permissive styles, including low demands for responsibility and a lack of parental oversight.

Permissive parents avoid punitive measures and allow children to engage in unacceptable activities and impulsive behaviors. These children are often neglected, and their emotional needs are not adequately attended to.

POINTS TO REMEMBER

Research consistently shows that parent-child communication about sex-related topics during adolescence can significantly reduce risky sexual behaviors, such as exposure to pornography, and sexually transmitted diseases (STDs).

Chapter 8

The Issues in Same-Gender Communication: Mothers Talk to Daughters, and Fathers Talk To Sons

The Importance of Open Communication About Sex

Talking to children about sex is a crucial aspect of their upbringing. While same-gender communication has its benefits, it should not be the only approach. Cross-gender conversations can be equally valuable and, in some cases, necessary to provide a well-rounded education. By adopting a balanced approach that includes comprehensive sex education and open dialogue, parents can equip their children with the knowledge and confidence they need to navigate their sexual development safely and healthily.

Breaking down the barriers to effective sex communication whether those barriers are based on gender, discomfort, or societal expectations will benefit not only individual families but society as a whole. When parents talk openly and honestly about sex, they help raise informed, responsible, and confident young people who are better prepared to make healthy choices throughout their lives.

Imagine a world where conversations about sexuality flow effortlessly between parents and children, where daughters can open up about their sexuality to their dads and sons to their moms. Such open communication could significantly reduce the rate of unwanted pregnancies and promote healthier sexual lives. However, sexuality is often acknowledged as a difficult topic, and in some families, it is rarely discussed. Many children remain silent on the subject, and consequently, parents may also refrain from initiating these conversations. Parents might assume their children already understand or feel uncertain about how to approach the subject.

Despite the recognized value of communication about sexuality, it is clear that mothers often bear most of the responsibility. Reasons for this include that mothers typically spend more time with the children, are perceived as better communicators, and are seen as agents of intimacy. Talking to children about sex is a vital aspect of their upbringing, yet there is little evidence that fathers have been integrated into mainstream thinking about family processes. What little research there is on father involvement usually relies on mothers when it comes to discussing sex and sexuality with children.

Many parents find themselves navigating a complex web of cultural norms, personal discomforts, and gender expectations. One striking aspect of this challenge is the tendency for same-gender communication: mothers talk to daughters, and fathers talk to sons. While common, this phenomenon raises important questions about how effectively parents can educate their children about sex and whether this practice truly serves the best interests of young people. By embracing a balanced approach that includes both same-gender and cross-gender conversations, parents can equip their children with the knowledge and confidence they need to navigate their sexual development safely and healthily.

The Real Issue

Effective communication is crucial in every aspect of our lives, but it's often the hardest skill to master. The responsibility for clear and open communication lies with everyone involved, not just one person. Whether discussing important health matters, sharing personal experiences, or simply expressing our thoughts and feelings, how we communicate can significantly impact our relationships and well-being.

Sarah, a 16-year-old high school student, shared her experiences in an interview. "Talking to my dad about my menstruation was awkward," she admitted. "I felt embarrassed and didn't know how to start the conversation. It was easier with my mom because she understood exactly what I was going through."

When it came to discussing her encounters with boys and the complexities of teenage relationships, Sarah found herself even more hesitant. "I wanted to talk about it, but I didn't think my dad would understand. It felt like there was this barrier between us."

Imagine a world where Sarah could openly discuss her sex life and relationships with her dad without feeling uncomfortable. A world where sons could talk to their mothers about their experiences and concerns with the same ease they might with their fathers. This ideal scenario emphasizes the importance of creating an environment where children feel safe and supported, regardless of the parent's gender. By fostering open, non-judgmental communication, parents can ensure their children receive the guidance and support they need to navigate their sexual development confidently and healthily.

POINTS TO REMEMBER

When it came to discussing her encounters with boys and the complexities of teenage relationships, Sarah found herself even more hesitant. "I wanted to talk about it, but I didn't think my dad would understand. It felt like there was this barrier between us."

Chapter 9

Barriers, Culture taboos, sexual silence,
Communication, and shyness

Why Is It So Difficult to Teach Sexual Health to Our Children?

Four major barriers have been identified to parent-adolescent communication about sex: limited sexual health knowledge, perceptions of adolescents' readiness for sex, parental comfort with discussing sex, and demographic factors. Additionally, Motsomi et al. (2016) highlighted other barriers, such as adolescents' misperceptions that guardians do not want to discuss sexual activities, strong belief systems of parents or guardians, myths that adolescents are too young, and cultural and religious beliefs.

When I asked parents about these challenges during my research, here are some of the responses I received:

Feeling Uncomfortable:

"Growing up in Africa, we didn't talk about it."

"With my son, even though he opened up to me, he was like, 'Oh, Mommy, I already know. So, you are weird. Why are you even talking to me about this?' He wasn't comfortable."

Uncertainty about What to Say:

"When we are talking, the children listen to us, and they see that we do not know. Yeah. Sometimes parents are clueless. The child doesn't even care about whatever you say."

These responses illustrate the complexities and discomforts parents face when trying to educate their children about sexual health.

A Father's Responses

"So, if I have to address menstruation, how will I do that? I wouldn't even go there. I don't know how to talk to someone about it."

"Regarding the menstrual issues they go through, their mom handles that."

"I think I'll focus on talking to my son about the things I know a guy should go through. With my daughter, I wouldn't know much to say, but I would just lay the groundwork with what I do know."

"You need to know what kind of words to use for your girls and also for your boys."

"I would say I know enough to answer some questions that might come up. But I'm still learning. I'm not there yet."

Parent-Child Gender Barriers

"Regarding menstrual stuff, I'm not sure what to do. I can tell my daughter to clean it up and stuff, but beyond that, I'm uncertain."

"I find it much easier to talk to my sons about sex than to my daughter. I would be more reserved in how I present sexual issues to my daughter compared to my sons."

Cultural Taboos

"Africans often view sexually related conversations as taboo. You will rarely see an African parent talking about sexual matters. When I lived with my parents, my father never discussed sexual matters with me. Africans tend to shy away from these discussions."

"Growing up, nobody talked to me about sexuality, and I had to figure it out myself. I made wrong choices and have come to understand that I cannot pretend these issues don't exist."

Lack of Knowledge or Parental Uncertainty

"Knowing what the right thing is to say and when to say it is challenging. Am I comfortable addressing these topics? No. For example, sometimes I might ask my son how many girlfriends he has or if he has any in his class, just to gauge his reaction. I end there because I'm clueless about what to say next, so it's been a challenge for me."

"When you don't know what's going on in their lives, you can't talk to them. Another parent noted that her son was not as receptive to discussing sex as her daughter."

Overcoming Barriers to Effective Parent-Child Communication

Effective parent-child communication is crucial for building a child's sense of self-worth, helping them resist peer pressure, preventing unplanned pregnancies, sexually transmitted diseases, and school dropout (Hacker et al., 2000). However, various barriers can impede this vital communication.

Families often face communication barriers due to factors such as sexual silence, cultural taboos, and shame, which prevent them from discussing sexual health with their children. Additionally, parents' lack of knowledge concerning sexual health can further hinder these conversations.

Studies have identified that cultural and communication barriers obstruct discussions between parents and adolescents regarding sexual health education. For instance, Christensen et al. (2017) found that many immigrant parents encounter cultural, traditional, or religious barriers that prevent meaningful conversations about sexuality. These barriers may include feelings of sexual shame, awkwardness, or embarrassment about the topic, lack of knowledge, and cultural or religious restrictions on the appropriateness of discussing sexual health.

Sexual Shame as a Barrier

Sexual shame is a significant barrier for many U.S. immigrant families, often rooted in family culture or beliefs. This is especially challenging for African couples, who may feel awkward, uncomfortable, and shy about initiating conversations related to sex with their children. These feelings can prevent effective communication.

Some researchers describe sexual shame as the intensely painful feeling or experience of believing we are flawed and therefore unworthy of acceptance and belonging due to our current or past sexual thoughts, experiences, or behaviors. Gordon (2018) expands on this by explaining that sexual shame is linked to an individual's sexual identity, attractions, feelings, and behaviors. Parker and Thomas (2009) noted that shame often produces a sense of badness or worthlessness, impacting mental health. Those who experience sexual shame may avoid seeking counseling or therapy, missing out on beneficial mental health.

In many U.S. immigrant families, sexual shame stems from family culture or beliefs. Parents play a crucial role in shaping their children's faith and values, modeling acceptable and non-acceptable conversations about sexuality. Understanding and addressing sexual shame is essential to fostering open and healthy communication about sexual health within families.

Culture as a Barrier

Culture, defined as the customs, identities, and behaviors of a particular nationality of people sustained through communication, actions, and interactions, plays a significant role in the communication of sexual health with children. Cultural factors impacting this communication include the belief that sex is shameful, parental embarrassment, and parents' lack of education to discuss sexuality.

Several cultural beliefs can hinder sexual health communication, such as the notion that sex education promotes promiscuity and premature exposure to sexual activity. Culture can greatly influence an individual's sexual identity, attitudes, and behaviors. For parent-child conversations about sexuality to be successful, culture must be considered. Culture significantly impacts learning about sexuality and the development of the sexual self.

Studies have indicated that various factors contribute to the development of young people's sexual health, including family structure, family connectedness, and parental monitoring.

Sexual Silence, Cultural Taboo, and Religiosity Contributing to Shame

- **Sexual Silence:** Sexual silence refers to the absence of open conversations about sexuality and relationships. This silence often leads to sexual shame, making it difficult for parents to initiate discussions about sexual matters with their children, including adolescents.

- **Cultural Taboo:** Taboos are cultural beliefs that stigmatize certain topics, actions, or ideas, resulting in shame, isolation, and stigmatization. In cultures where discussing sexuality and sexual health is forbidden, many girls and young women are unprepared for puberty. For example, studies show that some refugee women had no knowledge of menstruation before their first period and were unaware of pregnancy until they became pregnant. This lack of knowledge can lead to health issues. Some women describe their first menstruation as a painful and secretive experience, accompanied by anxiety and fear on their wedding nights.

- **Religiosity:** A high level of religiosity can reinforce these taboos and silences, contributing further to the sense of shame surrounding sexual topics.

Challenges in Menstruation Communication

Due to sexual silence and cultural taboos, menstruation, a natural reproductive process, is often associated with shame in certain cultures. As a result, it is rarely seen, discussed, or acknowledged.

Menstrual attitudes also influence sexual behavior. For instance, individuals who feel more comfortable discussing menstruation tend to have a higher awareness of sexuality than those who are uncomfortable with such conversations. Schooler et al. (2005) found that sexual shame linked to menstruation can affect women's overall approach to sexuality. Because attitudes towards menstruation are tied to broader views on sexuality, sexual shame and silence significantly shape girls' belief systems regarding sexuality.

Children Who Have Been Abused

Children who have been sexually abused often experience feelings of shame, guilt, and worthlessness. Perpetrators frequently induce blame and stigmatization, making it difficult for these children to trust others or discuss their ordeals.

Lack of Knowledge or Parental Uncertainty

Participant feedback on the lack of knowledge and uncertainty about what information to share with children supports both Research Question Two and Research Question Three. Regarding Research Question Three, the theme of lack of knowledge and parental uncertainty is pertinent to the perceptions of Sub-Saharan immigrant parents concerning communication barriers. According to the participants, many parents feel inadequately prepared to initiate and hold conversations with their children about sexuality and sexual matters.

POINTS TO REMEMBER

Studies have identified that cultural and communication barriers obstruct discussions between parents and adolescents regarding sexual health education.

Chapter 10

How to offer sexual health and relationship education (iCREATE) Method

Guide for Parents to Discuss "The Sex Talk" with Their Kids

Sex education is crucial during the formative years, particularly in pre-adolescence, when curiosity about sexual matters is essential for forming mature relationships with the opposite sex. Providing accurate information about sexual issues is especially important, as teenagers often become sexually active due to hormonal influences and may lack sufficient knowledge about their own sexual activity. Without the right information, teenagers may face significant mental health risks and make poor decisions influenced by misguided desires.

Sex education for teenagers should encompass more than just lessons on anatomy. It should also include understanding reproductive organs, identifying the signs of puberty and adulthood, and learning about sexual health. Parents play a vital role in this educational process. They should not hesitate to engage in open and honest dialogues with their children about various sexual issues. While it is important to teach religious and spiritual values related to sexuality, it is equally important to provide comprehensive education about sexuality itself.

Our reluctance to discuss sexuality with our children may stem from shyness, embarrassment, fear, shame, or worry, but it is a conversation that must be had for the well-being of our young people.

Young adult Muslims, in particular, often wish to have someone they trust, such as a parent, close relative, or Imam, discuss sexuality and relationships with them from an Islamic perspective. They have many questions about the physical, psychological, and emotional changes they experience during this period of life, but they are often afraid to ask.

It is imperative for parents to educate their teenagers on this issue. Without proper guidance, teenagers may turn to sources that do not align with Islamic values. As parents, it is our responsibility to invest in this aspect of their upbringing. Discussing sexuality is an integral part of their overall education and training. By engaging in these conversations, we can better prepare our young people for the changes they will face, thereby reducing their worry, anxiety, and fear.

As a parent, it is crucial to prepare your child for this stage of life. Unfortunately, free access to sexual content has become widespread among teenagers and children, primarily due to easily accessible media. Shows and images containing pornographic elements are widely available to children via their cell phones. This issue is exacerbated by parents who often consider sex to be a taboo topic, deeming it unimportant to educate their children about. In reality, sex education should begin at an early age.

In American society, pre-marital sex is prevalent, with seven out of ten teens having sex by age 19. This aligns with HEART's fieldwork, which involved over 2,000 women and girls nationwide. More than 60% of respondents reported dealing with depression, harmful behaviors such as eating disorders, cutting, substance abuse, bullying, and sexual experimentation, and expressed a desire for more information on these topics.

Misconception of Sex Education

There is a common misconception that comprehensive sex education, which includes information sexually transmitted diseases, and pregnancy, leads to increased promiscuity and early sexual activity. However, research shows the opposite. According to a 2010

Guttmacher Policy Review, there is no evidence that comprehensive sex education programs result in higher rates of sexual activity or earlier initiation. Instead, these programs can empower young people to delay sex and make more responsible decisions.

The most compelling reason for parents to discuss sex with their children is abstinence. Research indicates that parents significantly influence their teens' sexual behaviors. Teens are more likely to set sexual boundaries if their parents have discussed these topics with them. Additionally, other studies show that children who are comfortable talking about sex are more likely to delay sexual activity and be older when they first have intercourse.

A 2012 survey by the Office of Adolescent Health at the Department of Health and Human Services found that "almost 9 in 10 teens (87%) said that it would be much easier to postpone sexual activity and avoid pregnancy if they could have more open, honest conversations about these topics with their parents."

The Current State of Sex Education

Talking to your children about sexuality and finding the right words to answer their countless questions can be challenging. A limited focus on sex education is concerning from a public health perspective because it leaves youth unprepared to handle issues of reproductive and sexual health, leading to:

- Confusion, curiosity, and/or exploration due to being unprepared for bodily changes.

- Making uninformed decisions due to a lack of understanding of sexual health and its consequences.

- Seeking misinformation from pornographic magazines, internet sites, peers, or obscene jokes, perpetuating myths, misinformation, and unhealthy attitudes towards gender and sexuality.

- Relying on debunked cultural traditions, myths, and practices.

- Being unable to identify abuse and seek help.

- Having unhealthy sexual relationships in life or marriage, and succumbing to pressure to engage in sexual activity to fit in, even if not ready.

The absence of open dialogue and education about sexual health in the community leads to negative health outcomes, sexual experimentation, sexual violence, and marital challenges.

One of the challenges of starting this conversation is that historically, puberty and sex have been uncomfortable subjects across racial, ethnic, and religious communities. Strong notions of privacy, modesty, and shaming of sexual desire create an environment hostile to open discourse. While these conversations may be new for your family, it is essential to consider how everyone can be involved. Each family member should think about their comfort level with these conversations and even get creative with their approach.

Traditional Gender Roles

Traditionally, mothers talk to daughters while fathers talk to their sons. Although discussing sex may be uncomfortable for dads with daughters or mothers with sons, it is crucial for parents to engage in open, two-way conversations with all their children about sex. This approach models healthy communication about sensitive topics and encourages safe, healthy relationships. For example, a father who feels uncomfortable starting a face-to-face conversation might be more open to journal writing with his daughter to open up communication lines.

Let's Talk About the Guide

Remember, a well-informed child has a better chance of not becoming a victim of sexual abuse and is better prepared for the changes of puberty. The goal of emotional and sexual education is to sharpen children's critical thinking in the face of overexposure to sexuality. This guide offers practical steps for parents considering having these crucial conversations with their kids. The steps are easily memorable through the acronym iCREATE, which stands for:

By following the iCREATE model, parents can effectively guide their children through the complexities of sexual health and relationships while respecting cultural and religious values.

Step One: I – Intentional and Positive Interaction

What It Means

Intentional and positive interaction involves deliberately starting conversations on sensitive topics and maintaining a positive, non-judgmental tone.

- **Good Example:** A mother schedules regular one-on-one time with her daughter to discuss various life topics, including puberty and relationships, in a warm and supportive manner.

- **Bad Example:** A father only brings up the topic of sex after discovering his son watching inappropriate content online, leading to a heated and accusatory conversation.

Impact on Children

- **Positive Impact:** Children feel valued and understood, making them more likely to seek advice and guidance from their parents.

- **Negative Impact:** Children may feel ashamed or fearful, leading to secrecy and misinformation.

Step Two: C – Creating a Safe Place for Opportunities and Communication

What It Means

Creating a safe place means fostering an environment where children feel comfortable asking questions and expressing their thoughts without fear of judgment or punishment.

- **Good Example:** Parents openly discuss body changes and sexual health at the dinner table in a matter-of-fact way, ensuring no topic is off-limits.

- **Bad Example:** Parents avoid discussing sexual health entirely or respond with discomfort and avoidance when children bring it up.

Impact on Children

- **Positive Impact:** Children are more likely to share their concerns and seek guidance.

- **Negative Impact:** Children may turn to unreliable sources for information or internalize feelings of shame and confusion.

Step Three: R – Reflective Listening and Resources

What It Means

Reflective listening involves paying close attention to what your child is saying, validating their feelings, and providing accurate information and resources.

- **Good Example:** A mother listens attentively to her son's questions about puberty, acknowledges his feelings, and provides age-appropriate books and resources.

- **Bad Example:** A father dismisses his daughter's concerns about relationships and tells her to "figure it out on her own."

Impact on Children

- **Positive Impact:** Children feel heard and respected, fostering trust and openness.

- **Negative Impact:** Children may feel misunderstood and isolated, leading to poor decision-making.

Step Four: E – Empathy and Emotional Support

What It Means

Empathy and emotional support mean understanding and sharing the feelings of your child, providing comfort and reassurance during discussions about sensitive topics.

- **Good Example:** A mother recognizes her daughter's anxiety about body changes and reassures her that her feelings are normal, offering emotional support and understanding.

- **Bad Example:** A father dismisses his son's fears about puberty as silly, making him feel unsupported and invalidated.

Impact on Children

- **Positive Impact:** Children feel emotionally supported and understood which builds their confidence and emotional resilience.

- **Negative Impact:** Children may feel alienated and unsupported, leading to increased anxiety and insecurity.

Emotional Support and Sexual Health

Emotional support plays a crucial role in fostering healthy sexual behaviors. Parents should reassure their children that they can approach them with any concerns or questions without fear of criticism. This support builds trust and encourages ongoing dialogue. The emotional and instrumental support provided during these conversations is essential. Adolescents who perceive their parents as supportive and non-judgmental are more likely to engage in open discussions about sexuality. According to Brody et al. (1998), youths who feel their parents will listen without criticism are more inclined to seek their guidance on sexual matters.

For example, imagine a scenario where a father notices his teenage daughter feeling anxious about attending a school dance. Instead of imposing strict rules or showing disapproval, he sits down with her, shares stories from his own adolescence, and discusses the importance of making safe choices. This supportive approach not only eases her anxiety but also instills confidence in her to make responsible decisions.

Examples of Emotional Support and Impact on Children:

- **Good Example:** A mother hugs her daughter and expresses understanding when she shares her anxiety about growing up and peer pressure.

- **Bad Example:** A father reacts with anger and frustration when his son confides in him about peer pressure to engage in sexual activities.

Impact on Children

- **Positive Impact:** Children feel supported and are more likely to approach parents with their problems.

- **Negative Impact:** Children may feel rejected and unsupported, increasing the risk of harmful behaviors.

Step Five: A – Attitudes and Asking Questions

What It Means

Having a positive and open attitude towards discussions about sex and sexuality, and encouraging children to ask questions and express their views.

- **Good Example:** Parents regularly ask their children about their thoughts and feelings regarding relationships and sexuality, and answer their questions patiently.

- **Bad Example:** Parents avoid the topic altogether or shut down questions with statements like "You're too young to know about this."

Impact on Children

- **Positive Impact:** Children feel their opinions are valued and are more likely to engage in open dialogue.

- **Negative Impact:** Children may feel discouraged from seeking information and advice from their parents.

Engaging children in home-based sex education involves asking open-ended questions that encourage critical thinking, curiosity, and dialogue. Here are some revised examples to get the conversation started:

1. **Body Awareness:**

   - "Can you name different body parts?"

   - "What do you know about how our bodies change as we grow?"

   - "Why do you think it's important to take care of our bodies?"

2. **Personal Boundaries:**

   - "How do you feel about personal space and privacy?"

   - "What are some ways we can show respect for other people's bodies?"

   - "Why is it important to say 'no' if we don't feel comfortable with something?"

3. **Reproductive Anatomy:**

   - "Can you identify the parts of the body involved in making babies?"

   - "What do you know about how babies are made?"

   - "How do boys' bodies differ from girls' bodies?"

4. **Relationships and Communication:**

   - "What does it mean to be a good friend?"

- "How do you think people should treat each other in a relationship?"

- "Why is it important to talk openly and honestly with people we care about?"

5. **Understanding Emotions:**

   - "What are some different feelings people might have when they're in love?"

   - "How can we tell if someone likes us or if we like someone?"

   - "What do you think it means to have a crush on someone?"

6. **Consent and Respect:**

   - "What does 'consent' mean to you?"

   - "Why is it important to ask for permission before touching someone else?"

   - "What are some ways we can show respect for other people's boundaries?"

7. **Media Literacy:**

   - "Have you seen or heard anything about relationships or bodies in movies or on the internet?"

- "How do you think the media influences our ideas about sex and relationships?"

- "What do you think is realistic or unrealistic about the way sex is portrayed in the media?"

8. **Safety and Responsibility:**

   - "What are some ways we can stay safe online?"

   - "What should we do if someone online tries to talk to us about things that make us uncomfortable?"

   - "How can we make sure we're ready for certain experiences before we have them?"

9. **Values and Beliefs:**

   - "What do you think our family's values are when it comes to relationships and sex?"

   - "How do you think our beliefs about sex and relationships are similar to or different from those of other families?"

   - "Why do you think people have different opinions about sex?"

10. **Encouraging Questions:**

    - "Is there anything about bodies, relationships, or feelings that you're curious about or want to learn more about?"

- "Do you have any questions about anything we've talked about today?"

- "What's something you've heard or seen that you'd like to talk about?"

These questions serve as starting points for meaningful conversations about sex education at home, enabling children to explore their thoughts, feelings, and curiosities in a safe and supportive environment.

Step 6: T – Teaching Moments for Engagement

What It Means

Using everyday situations and media as opportunities to teach and engage children about sexual health and relationships.

- **Good Example:** Parents use a TV show scene involving a romantic relationship to discuss healthy relationships and consent with their children.

- **Bad Example:** Parents ignore or turn off the TV when such scenes appear, missing the opportunity to educate.

Impact on Children

- **Positive Impact:** Children learn to critically analyze media and understand real-life implications of relationships.

- **Negative Impact:** Children may develop misconceptions based on unfiltered media portrayals.

This approach encourages parents to actively use everyday occurrences and media exposure as teaching moments, fostering a deeper understanding of sexual health and relationships in their children.

Teaching moments provide excellent opportunities to impart sex education to your child in a natural and meaningful way. Here's how you can use everyday situations as teaching moments:

1. **Bathing or Dressing:** While helping your child bathe or get dressed, casually talk about body parts using their correct names. Explain the importance of privacy and boundaries, such as not touching others' private parts and respecting personal space.

2. **Watching TV or Movies:** If you come across a scene in a TV show or movie that involves relationships or sexuality, use it as a teaching moment. Discuss the emotions involved, the importance of communication and consent, and compare how relationships are portrayed in media to real life.

3. **Pregnancy and Birth:** If you or someone close to you is expecting a baby, talk about pregnancy and childbirth. Explain how babies grow inside the mother's womb and how they are born. Discuss the roles of parents in caring for a newborn.

4. **Observing Animals:** If you observe animals mating or caring for their young, use it to explain reproduction and parenting. Discuss how different species reproduce and emphasize the importance of caring for offspring.

5. **Answering Curious Questions:** Children are naturally curious, so be prepared to answer their questions about sex and reproduction when they arise. Use age-appropriate language and provide honest, accurate information. Encourage them to ask questions and assure them that no question is off-limits.

6. **Discussing Relationships:** Emphasize the importance of mutual respect, communication, and consent when discussing relationships with your child. Talk about what makes a healthy relationship and how to recognize warning signs of unhealthy dynamics.

7. **Addressing Peer Influence:** If your child hears misinformation or inappropriate language from peers, use it as an opportunity to correct misconceptions. Reinforce your family's values and beliefs about sex and relationships.

8. **Internet Safety:** Teach your child about internet safety, including responsible online behavior and avoiding exposure to inappropriate material. Discuss the risks of sharing personal

information online and how to handle encounters with strangers.

9. **Discussing Changes in Puberty:** As your child approaches puberty, discuss the physical and emotional changes they will experience. Explain hormonal changes, menstruation (for girls), and other biological aspects of puberty in an age-appropriate manner.

10. **Setting Boundaries:** Use everyday interactions to reinforce the importance of setting and respecting boundaries. Teach your child to assert themselves when uncomfortable and to respect others' boundaries.

These strategies ensure that sex education conversations are integrated naturally into everyday life, helping children develop a healthy understanding of sexual health and relationships.

Step Seven: E – Establish Ongoing Communication

What It Means

Establishing an ongoing dialogue rather than having a single "talk," ensuring that children know they can come to their parents anytime with questions or concerns.

- **Good Example:** Parents regularly check in with their children about their lives, including topics related to sexual health and relationships.

- **Bad Example:** Parents have one serious conversation about sex and never revisit the topic again.

Impact on Children

- **Positive Impact:** Children feel continuous support and guidance, leading to informed and safe decision-making.

- **Negative Impact:** Children may feel abandoned or unsupported after the initial conversation, potentially leading to risks and misinformation.

Establishing ongoing communication fosters trust and ensures that children receive consistent guidance as they navigate issues related to sexual health and relationships.

POINTS TO REMEMBER

Good Example: A mother schedules regular one-on-one time with her daughter to discuss various life topics, including puberty and relationships, in a warm and supportive manner.

Bad Example: A father only brings up the topic of sex after discovering his son watching inappropriate content online, leading to a heated and accusatory conversation.

Chapter 11

―――――∧―――――

Teaching your teenagers to build
healthy relationships

Adolescence is often considered a challenging transitional period for both children and parents. Teenagers are searching for their identity, dealing with peer pressure, and facing increasing academic challenges. Amidst the whirlwind of high school, social media, and evolving friendships, teenagers are also beginning to explore romantic relationships. As a parent, guiding your teen through these formative years is crucial for helping them develop healthy relationship skills.

The Importance of Healthy Communication

Fostering open and honest conversation with your teen increases the likelihood that they will come to you to discuss important matters, such as relationships, school, sex, and drugs, rather than turning to friends or feeling isolated. Let's begin with the most important aspect:

1. Communication: The Foundation of Healthy Relationships

Effective communication is the cornerstone of any healthy relationship. Teaching your teenager how to communicate openly, honestly, and respectfully is vital. It's important to help your teenager understand that words and actions have a lasting impact. Once spoken, words cannot be taken back. Encourage your teenager to choose their words carefully by asking themselves:

- Will my words hurt or uplift the other person?

- Is what I'm about to say kind and respectful?

- Am I expressing myself clearly and honestly?

It's also crucial to teach your teenager that rejection and arguments are normal parts of relationships. By paying attention to their words and maintaining a calm demeanor, they can help prevent conflicts from escalating.

Practical Advice for Parents

- **Be a Role Model:** As the saying goes, you cannot preach what you don't practice. As parents, our behavior and actions significantly impact our children. It's crucial to be good and positive role models by practicing the values we teach, such as politeness, hard work, and integrity. Admitting and learning from our mistakes teaches teens responsibility and the importance of personal growth.

- **Encourage Active Listening:** Teach your teen to listen without interrupting and to acknowledge the other person's perspective. Role-play scenarios where they practice repeating back what the other person said to ensure understanding.

- **Body Language and Tone:** Remind your teenager that communication is not just about words. Nonverbal cues like body language and tone of voice also play a significant role. Encourage them to be mindful of these cues to enhance their communication skills and relationships.

2. Conflict Management: Navigating Disagreements Constructively

During adolescence, many teens experience romantic and intimate relationships for the first time. While these relationships bring many positive elements into their lives, they also introduce the challenge of managing disagreements and conflicts.

Conflict is inevitable in any relationship. It's a common misconception that in these situations, the man is always the perpetrator and the woman the victim. Multiple investigations reveal that violence, especially non-sexual violence among dating adolescent couples, often involves mutual exchanges of aggression.

In 2020, the Centers for Disease Control and Prevention (CDC) reported that about 12% of dating adolescent couples experienced conflict situations. A study conducted in 2008 on a sample of 4,667 young people aged 13 to 18 found that 25% to 30% of American youth had been victims of violence in their intimate relationships. Common causes of conflict include insecurity, poor communication, unmet needs, and lack of trust. Additionally, consumption habits, such as drug and alcohol use, can also contribute to conflicts among adolescents.

Teaching your teen how to manage conflicts constructively can help them maintain healthy relationships. Here's how:

- **Understanding the Causes of Conflict:** Help your teen recognize the root causes of conflicts, such as insecurity, poor communication, unmet needs, and lack of trust. Discuss how consumption habits, like drug and alcohol use, can exacerbate these issues.

- **Promoting Healthy Communication:** Encourage open and honest dialogue where both parties feel heard. Teach your teen to express their feelings without blaming or attacking the other person.

- **Developing Conflict Resolution Skills:** Introduce conflict resolution techniques, such as active listening, finding common ground, and compromising. Role-playing different scenarios can be a practical way for teens to practice these skills.

- **Emphasizing Empathy:** Teach your teen to consider the other person's perspective and to respond with empathy and understanding. This approach can de-escalate conflicts and foster a supportive environment.

- **Setting Boundaries:** Help your teen establish and respect personal boundaries in their relationships. Understanding and maintaining boundaries is crucial for healthy interactions and preventing conflicts from escalating.

- **Seeking Support:** Encourage your teen to seek support from trusted adults, such as parents, teachers, or counselors, when they face challenging situations in their relationships.

By equipping your teen with these conflict management skills, you can help them navigate disagreements constructively and maintain healthy, positive relationships.

Practical Advice:

In a relationship, it is impossible to avoid disagreements. These conflicts can help us understand each other better, provide opportunities to express our needs, and ultimately strengthen our bond. As parents, it's important to teach your teen that disagreements can be constructive rather than destructive. Here's how you can guide them:

- **Normalize Disagreements:** Explain that disagreements are normal and occur in all relationships, whether they are friendships, romantic relationships, or family bonds. They don't signify something is wrong; instead, they are opportunities to understand each other better.

Example: "Your dad and I often disagree about how to spend our weekends. He prefers staying home and relaxing, while I like to go out and explore new places."

- **Learning Opportunity:** Highlight that disagreements can teach valuable lessons about each other's perspectives and preferences. Encourage your teen to see these moments as opportunities to learn and grow together rather than as battles to be won.

Example: "Initially, these disagreements used to frustrate both of us because we couldn't understand each other's points of view. But over time, we've learned that these differences actually help us learn more about each other."

- **Finding Common Ground:** Encourage your teen to seek common ground and compromise. Discuss the importance of respecting each other's preferences while also finding ways to meet both parties' needs.

Example: "Our relationship has become stronger because we've learned to appreciate each other's preferences and find ways to make both of us happy."

3. Emotional Regulation: Managing Emotions in Adolescents

Managing emotions is a critical skill for conflict resolution among adolescents. Teenagers often experience intense and conflicting emotions, which can complicate their ability to navigate conflicts effectively. As a parent, supporting your teen in developing emotional regulation skills is essential for fostering peaceful and productive interactions.

Here are effective strategies to assist your teen in managing their emotions:

- **Identify and Name Emotions:** Encourage your teen to identify and label their emotions. Simply acknowledging what they are feeling can enhance their self-awareness and enable them to respond more thoughtfully.

- **Teach Relaxation Techniques:** Introduce relaxation methods such as deep breathing or meditation. These techniques can help your teen calm themselves when overwhelmed by emotions.

- **Promote Healthy Expression:** Encourage your teen to express their emotions in a healthy and respectful manner. It's crucial they learn to communicate their feelings without resorting to aggression or verbal abuse.

- **Model Healthy Emotional Management:** Serve as a role model by demonstrating constructive ways to manage your own emotions. This modeling helps them recognize that emotions are natural and can be effectively managed.

By supporting your teen in these ways, you can equip them with valuable skills that contribute to their emotional well-being and their ability to handle conflicts positively.

4. Resisting Sexual Coercion and Pressure

Sexual coercion, as defined by Abbey et al. (2014), refers to the use of any tactic or strategy aimed at engaging another person in sexual behavior against their will. This term encompasses a wide range of manipulative tactics designed to pressure someone into a sexual relationship. According to Benbouriche and Parent (2018), understanding these tactics is crucial for recognizing and resisting them.

French et al. (2015) identify three primary types of sexual coercion:

1. **Psychological Coercion:** This involves using pressure, threats, or blackmail. Examples include putting pressure on someone, belittling them, or harassing them to compel them into a sexual act.

2. **Physical Coercion:** This involves the use of force or authority to obtain compliance.

3. **Coercion by Alcohol or Drugs:** This tactic exploits the impairment caused by alcohol or drugs. For instance, some men believe that women who drink are more sexually available and thus persist longer in pressuring them for sex if they observe that a woman has consumed alcohol.

Understanding these forms of coercion is essential for both recognizing when they occur and knowing how to resist them effectively.

Sexual Coercion: Traumatic Impacts

1. Psychological Effects:

- Trauma from sexual coercion can affect desire, arousal, and sexual performance.

- It can result in negative emotions, mental health issues, and suicidal ideation.

2. Behavioral Effects:

- Women may exhibit internalized behaviors such as depression and withdrawal.

- Men may display externalized behaviors such as aggression and antisocial actions.

- Victims may struggle with intimate relationships due to traumatic memories of past violence.

3. Impact on Sexuality:

- Female victims may use sex as a means of emotional regulation and self-esteem, leading to more frequent engagement in casual sex.

- Coercive experiences often result in feelings of exploitation, vulnerability, betrayal, and shame, violating the right to consensual sexual activity.

4. Broader Mental Health Effects:

- Sexual violence is associated with higher rates of anxiety disorders, social anxiety, panic disorders, and agoraphobia.

- It can disrupt attachment and intimate relationships due to changes in the hypothalamic-pituitary-adrenal (HPA) axis.

5. Influence of Individual and Social Factors:

- Factors such as resilience, social support, and genetics can influence the development and persistence of these reactions.

Parents play a critical role in addressing and preventing such trauma. By equipping their teenage children with knowledge, confidence, and strategies, parents can help them resist sexual coercion and pressure.

Here are some essential guidelines for parents, backed by compelling examples:

1. Open Communication: Create an environment where teens feel safe to share their thoughts and experiences without fear of judgment or punishment. This involves listening actively and responding empathetically. For example, you might say, "I want you to know that you can talk to me about anything, including relationships and sex. I'm here to listen and help without judgment." This approach establishes trust and ensures your teen feels comfortable seeking your advice.

2. Recognize Coercive Behaviors: Understand the tactics people use to manipulate others into sexual activities against their will, such as guilt-tripping, threats, or persistent pressure. Avoid dismissive attitudes like "Boys will be boys" or "It's just part of dating." Instead, teach your teens to identify and resist manipulative tactics by explaining, "If someone tries to guilt-trip you or uses phrases like 'If you loved me, you would,' that's manipulation. You have the right to set boundaries and say no."

3. Build Self-Esteem: Help teens develop a positive self-image and confidence in their abilities and worth. Encourage involvement in activities that build confidence and support their interests and autonomy. For example, you might say, "I believe in your abilities and decisions. Pursue what makes you happy and strong." This helps them resist peer pressure and make autonomous decisions.

4. Develop Assertiveness Skills: Instead of simply telling teens to "just say no," provide practical ways to do so. Teach and practice assertive communication by role-playing scenarios where they might feel pressured. Show them how to firmly state their boundaries, saying, "If you're ever pressured, look them in the eye and say firmly, 'I'm not comfortable with that.' Let's practice it together now."

5. Create a Support System: Ensure that teens have a network of trusted adults and peers they can turn to for advice and support. Make sure your teen knows they have a support network by saying, "If you ever feel uncomfortable or pressured, you can always talk to me, your aunt, or your coach. We're all here for you."

6. Understand Healthy Relationships: Teach the characteristics of respectful, supportive, and balanced relationships versus those that are manipulative or abusive. Watch shows or movies together and discuss them, saying, "See how this character respects their partner's boundaries? That's what a healthy relationship looks like."

7. Safety Planning: Create strategies for teens to use if they find themselves in uncomfortable or dangerous situations, such as having exit plans and knowing who to call for help. Establish a safety plan, like a family code word for emergencies. Tell your teen, "If you ever need an excuse to leave a situation, text this word, and I'll call you immediately with an emergency."

By following these guidelines, parents can empower their teens to resist sexual coercion and pressure, fostering their ability to make safe and healthy decisions.

1. Avoiding Dating Violence

Sexual Violence refers to any act that degrades insults, harasses, and/or attacks a person's body and/or reproductive functions due to unequal power relations and/or gender, resulting in psychological and/or physical suffering. This includes disrupting a person's reproductive health and hindering their ability to pursue education safely and optimally.

Sexual violence is prevalent in everyday life, occurring within families, communities, schools, and workplaces. According to data from the Ministry of Women's Empowerment and Child Protection, Indonesia recorded 11,686 cases of sexual violence in 2022. The majority of victims are women, highlighting a significant gender disparity.

Research published on November 1 in the Journal of Interpersonal Violence reveals that adolescents who share a strong, positive bond with their mothers are more likely to avoid violent relationships later in life, even if the mother herself has experienced a conflicted relationship. Livingston, the lead researcher, notes, "Parents who have developed effective conflict resolution skills pass those skills on to their children, which ultimately impacts their relationships throughout their lives."

Dating Violence Among Youth:

- Dating violence affects approximately 1 in 3 teens in relationships, with severity and frequency varying greatly among individuals.

- The effects of youth dating violence can be both immediate and long-lasting, often persisting beyond adolescence and worsening over time.

- Youth dating violence places young people at risk of physical, mental, and social health problems.

Addressing and preventing dating violence is crucial for the well-being of young people and the broader community. It requires fostering healthy relationships, promoting effective conflict resolution skills, and ensuring safe environments for education and personal development.

Signs Your Teen Might Be in an Abusive Relationship

- **Loss of Interest in Activities:** Your teenager is losing interest in activities they previously enjoyed.

- **Increased Isolation:** Your teenager is no longer seeing friends and family members and is becoming increasingly isolated.

- **Control by Partner:** Your teen's partner controls their behavior, constantly monitoring them, calling frequently, and demanding to know who they have been with.

- **Casual Mentions of Abuse:** Your teen casually mentions their partner's abusive behavior but laughs it off as a joke.

- **Unexplained Injuries:** Your teen often has unexplained injuries or provides explanations that don't make sense.

- **Partner's Violent Temper:** You witness your teen's partner losing their temper violently, hitting, or breaking things.

Practical Advice:

Establish Open Communication

- **Good Approach:** Create a safe, non-judgmental space for your teen to discuss their feelings and experiences. Regularly check in with them about their relationships and listen without interrupting.

  - **Example:** "Every week, let's have some time to talk about anything you want. I'm here to listen and support you, no matter what."

- **Bad Approach:** Dismissing or belittling their feelings when they try to open up.

- Example: "You're too young to know what real problems are. Just focus on your studies."

Educate About Healthy Relationships

- **Good Approach**: Discuss the characteristics of healthy and unhealthy relationships. Explain the importance of mutual respect, trust, and equality.

  - Example: "Healthy relationships are built on trust and respect. Both partners should feel safe and valued."

- **Bad Approach**: Assuming your teen already knows what a healthy relationship looks like without providing guidance.

  - Example: "You should know what's right and wrong by now."

Recognize Warning Signs of Abuse

- **Good Approach**: Teach your teen the signs of dating violence and encourage them to trust their instincts if something feels wrong.

  - Example: "If someone is controlling, isolating, or hurting you, that's not love. Trust your feelings and talk to me if you notice these signs."

- **Bad Approach**: Ignoring changes in your teen's behavior or dismissing their concerns as typical teenage drama.

- o **Example:** "All teens go through phases. You're just being dramatic."

Build Self-Esteem and Empowerment

- **Good Approach:** Support your teen in activities that build their self-worth and confidence. Encourage them to pursue their interests and passions.

  - o **Example:** "I love how dedicated you are to your art. It's amazing to see you grow and express yourself."

- **Bad Approach:** Criticizing their choices or comparing them to others.

  - o **Example:** "Why can't you be more like your sibling who is so focused on their studies?"

Develop Conflict Resolution Skills

- **Good Approach:** Model and teach effective conflict resolution skills. Show how to handle disagreements calmly and respectfully.

  - o **Example:** "Let's talk about how we can solve this issue together. Finding a solution that works for both of us is important."

- **Bad Approach:** Demonstrating aggressive or dismissive behavior during conflicts.

- Example: "Just do as I say. I don't have time to argue with you."

Foster a Strong Bond

- **Good Approach:** Build a positive, supportive relationship with your teen. This bond can serve as a buffer against violent relationships later in life.

  - Example: "Remember, I'm always here for you, no matter what. We can get through anything together."

- **Bad Approach:** Being emotionally distant or unavailable, which can leave your teen feeling unsupported?

  - Example: "I'm too busy with work. Handle your problems on your own."

Safety Planning

- **Good Approach:** Help your teen create a safety plan if they ever feel threatened or unsafe. Discuss steps they can take to protect themselves.

  - Example: "If you ever feel unsafe, you can text me a code word, and I'll come get you immediately, no questions asked."

- **Bad Approach:** Assuming your teen will never face such situations and not discussing safety plans.

o **Example:** "You don't need a safety plan. Just use common sense."

By using these approaches, parents can provide comprehensive guidance to help their teens avoid dating violence. The goal is to empower them with the knowledge, skills, and confidence to recognize unhealthy behaviors and seek help when needed.

2. Developing Personality and Character Qualities

Building a strong, positive personality and developing essential character qualities are crucial aspects of a teenager's growth. These traits influence how they interact with others, face challenges, and navigate relationships throughout their lives. Parents play a significant role in guiding their teens to develop these qualities effectively.

Research into parenting styles has consistently shown that adolescents are less likely to suffer from anxiety or depression, or to abuse drugs or alcohol, when parents are warm, respectful, and supportive, and hold consistent, firm, and rational expectations for behavior. These adolescents are also more likely to exhibit maturity, resilience, optimism, self-regulation, and perform better academically compared to their peers whose parents lack warmth or clear expectations (or both).

The quality of the parent-adolescent relationship significantly influences the development of these positive traits. For instance, adolescents who report satisfaction with their relationship with their parents, and who frequently discuss topics related to love, sexual relationships, and safe sex, are more likely to delay sexual activity, even in the face of peer pressure. Furthermore, good rapport between parents and adolescents, combined with reasonable parental monitoring, has been shown to protect against adolescent substance use.

Practical Advice

Helping your teen develop strong personality and character qualities can contribute to healthier relationships. Here are some practical steps:

Recognize Warning Signs of Trouble

- **Good Approach:** Teach your teen the signs of unhealthy behavior and encourage them to trust their instincts if something feel wrong.

  - **Example:** "If someone is controlling, isolating, or hurting you, that's not normal. Trust your feelings and talk to me if you notice these signs."

- **Bad Approach:** Ignoring changes in your teen's behavior or dismissing their concerns as typical teenage drama.

  - **Example:** "All teens go through phases. You're just being dramatic."

Build Self-Esteem and Empowerment

- **Good Approach:** Support your teen in activities that build their self-worth and confidence. Encourage them to pursue their interests and passions.

  o **Example:** "I love how dedicated you are to your art. It's amazing to see you grow and express yourself."

- **Bad Approach:** Criticizing their choices or comparing them to others.

  o **Example:** "Why can't you be more like your sibling who is so focused on their studies?"

Foster Critical Thinking and Problem-Solving

- **Good Approach:** Encourage your teen to think critically about situations and develop problem-solving skills. Discuss various scenarios and possible solutions together.

  o **Example:** "What do you think is the best way to handle this conflict with your friend? Let's brainstorm some ideas."

- **Bad Approach:** Solving problems for your teen without involving them in the process.

  o **Example:** "I'll take care of this issue with your teacher; you don't need to worry about it."

Encourage Resilience and Perseverance

- **Good Approach:** Teach your teen to bounce back from setbacks and keep trying despite difficulties. Celebrate their efforts and progress, not just their successes.

  o **Example:** "I know you didn't make the team this time, but I'm proud of how hard you worked. Let's keep practicing and try again next year."

- **Bad Approach:** Focusing only on outcomes and not the effort put in, or discouraging them from trying again after a failure.

  o **Example:** "You didn't make the team, so maybe you should focus on something else instead."

Promote Healthy Lifestyle Choices

- **Good Approach:** Encourage your teen to take care of their physical and mental health through regular exercise, balanced nutrition, and adequate rest.

  o **Example:** "Let's plan our meals for the week to include lots of fruits and vegetables, and find a fun activity we can do together to stay active."

- **Bad Approach:** Ignoring the importance of a healthy lifestyle or not modeling healthy behaviors yourself.

o **Example:** "Just eat whatever you want; it doesn't really matter."

3. Balancing Attraction with Values

Teaching your teen to balance physical attraction with their values is essential for fostering healthier relationship choices. Understanding and navigating the complexities of attraction while staying true to one's values can help prevent relationship pitfalls and promote emotional well-being.

Ultimately, while the thrill of attraction is undeniable, it is the alignment of values that determines the depth and longevity of a relationship. By prioritizing values alongside attraction, individuals can build relationships that are not only passionate but also enduring, supportive, and fulfilling.

Practical Advice

Teaching your teen to balance physical attraction with their values can help them make healthier relationship choices. Here's how to do it:

Reflect on Attraction

- **Good Approach:** Discuss the difference between physical attraction and a deeper connection. Explain that while attraction is natural, lasting relationships are built on shared values and mutual respect.

- Example: "It's normal to be attracted to someone's looks, but it's their character that will matter in the long run."

- **Bad Approach:** Ignoring the topic of attraction entirely.

  - Example: "Looks don't matter at all; focus only on character."

Recognize Personal Values

- **Good Approach:** Help your teen identify what is truly important to them in a relationship. This can include traits like respect, honesty, and kindness.

  - Example: "Take some time to think about what qualities you admire in friends and family. These are the same qualities that should matter in a partner."

- **Bad Approach:** Assuming your teen already understands their values without discussing them.

  - Example: "You know what's right and wrong; you don't need to think about it."

Recognize Unhealthy Behaviors

- **Good Approach:** Help your teen understand the signs of an unhealthy relationship, such as controlling behavior, isolation, or any form of abuse.

- o **Example:** "If someone is trying to control your actions or isolate you from friends, that's a red flag. Trust your gut feelings about these situations."

- **Bad Approach:** Downplaying or ignoring these signs.

  - o **Example:** "Everyone gets jealous sometimes; it's no big deal."

Foster Independence

- **Good Approach:** Promote independence and self-reliance. Help your teen feel empowered to make their own choices and stand by their values.

  - o **Example:** "Trust yourself to make decisions that align with your values, even if others might disagree."

- **Bad Approach:** Making decisions for them or undermining their choices.

  - o **Example:** "I know what's best for you; just do what I say."

4. Developing and Defining Sexual Values and Boundaries

Parents play a critical role in helping their teenagers develop and define their sexual values and boundaries.

Sexual values and boundaries are the principles and limits individuals set regarding their sexual behavior and relationships. These values reflect personal beliefs about sex, intimacy, and respect, while boundaries define what is acceptable and unacceptable in a relationship. Teaching teens to balance physical attraction with their values can help them make healthier relationship choices and avoid harmful situations.

Self-awareness is crucial for teens to understand their own values and what they seek in a relationship. Parents can support this by encouraging their teens to reflect on their beliefs and aspirations. For example, parents might ask their teens to consider questions like, "What qualities do you value in a partner?" and "How do you want to be treated in a relationship?" These reflections can help teens establish clear boundaries and recognize when those boundaries are being respected or violated.

Physical attraction is a natural part of adolescence, but it's essential for teens to balance this with their values. Parents can guide their teens by discussing the difference between attraction and meaningful connection. Emphasize that a healthy relationship should align with their values and boundaries, not just physical desires.

By supporting their teens in developing and defining their sexual values and boundaries, parents can help them make informed and respectful decisions about their relationships.

Practical Advice for Parents

Establish Open Communication

- **Good Approach:** Create a safe, non-judgmental space for your teen to discuss their feelings and experiences. Regularly check in with them about their relationships and listen without interrupting.

  - **Example:** "Every week, let's have some time to talk about anything you want. I'm here to listen and support you, no matter what."

- **Bad Approach:** Dismissing or belittling their feelings when they try to open up.

  - **Example:** "You're too young to know what real problems are. Just focus on your studies."

Educate About Healthy Relationships

- **Good Approach:** Discuss the characteristics of healthy and unhealthy relationships. Explain the importance of mutual respect, trust, and equality.

  - **Example:** "Healthy relationships are built on trust and respect. Both partners should feel safe and valued."

- **Bad Approach:** Assuming your teen already knows what a healthy relationship looks like without providing guidance.

- Example: "You should know what's right and wrong by now."

Recognize Warning Signs of Abuse

- **Good Approach:** Teach your teen the signs of dating violence and encourage them to trust their instincts if something feel wrong.

  - **Example:** "If someone is controlling, isolating, or hurting you, that's not love. Trust your feelings and talk to me if you notice these signs."

- **Bad Approach:** Ignoring changes in your teen's behavior or dismissing their concerns as typical teenage drama.

  - **Example:** "All teens go through phases. You're just being dramatic."

Build Self-Esteem and Empowerment

- **Good Approach:** Support your teen in activities that build their self-worth and confidence. Encourage them to pursue their interests and passions.

  - **Example:** "I love how dedicated you are to your art. It's amazing to see you grow and express yourself."

- **Bad Approach:** Criticizing their choices or comparing them to others.

○ **Example:** "Why can't you be more like your sibling who is so focused on their studies?"

In addition, provide accurate information: Ensure your teen has access to reliable information about sexual health and safety.

5. Attitudes That Make Relationships Work

You've likely heard the famous quote, "Attitude is everything." This is especially true when it comes to human interactions. Whether it's connections between siblings, family members, spiritual acquaintances, or romantic partners, attitude plays a crucial role in the success of these relationships.

For teenagers, cultivating the right attitudes can lay the foundation for healthy and fulfilling relationships. Parents play a pivotal role in guiding their teens towards developing these positive attitudes. By fostering open communication, mutual respect, empathy, and resilience, parents can help their teens build strong, supportive relationships that can withstand the challenges of adolescence and beyond.

The **Importance** of Attitude in Relationships

Attitude influences how individuals perceive and react to their partners and the situations they encounter. Positive attitudes such as optimism, empathy, and respect contribute to healthier and more satisfying relationships. Conversely, negative attitudes like cynicism, jealousy, and disrespect can undermine even the strongest bonds. For teenagers, whose relationships are often characterized by intense emotions and rapid changes, maintaining a positive attitude is particularly crucial.

Practical Advice for Parents

Here are some practical steps parents can take to foster positive attitudes in their teens:

Model Positive Attitudes

- **Demonstrate empathy, respect, and effective communication in your own relationships.** Teens learn a lot by observing their parents' interactions and attitudes.

  - **Example:** When resolving conflicts with your partner, show how to handle disagreements respectfully and constructively. Explain to your teen how both parties can work through issues without resorting to anger or disrespect.

- **Ineffective Example:** Arguing loudly and disrespectfully in front of your teen, which can set a negative example and normalize unhealthy conflict resolution?

Educate About Healthy Relationships

Positive Approaches

- **Discuss the characteristics of healthy and unhealthy relationships.** Explain the importance of mutual respect, trust, and equality.

  o **Example:** "Healthy relationships are built on trust and respect. Both partners should feel safe and valued."

- **Inadequate Approach:** Assuming your teen already knows what a healthy relationship looks like without providing guidance.

  o **Example:** "You should know what's right and wrong by now."

Discuss Real-Life Scenarios

- **Use real-life examples and scenarios to discuss the importance of positive attitudes in relationships.** Talk about how different attitudes can impact relationships, both positively and negatively.

  o **Example:** Share stories about relationships where positive attitudes like patience and empathy made a difference. Discuss characters from books, movies, or TV shows to highlight how attitudes shape relationships.

- **Ineffective Example:** Avoiding discussions about relationships, leaving your teen to learn about them from less reliable sources or through trial and error without guidance.

Encourage Reflection

- **Help your teen reflect on their own attitudes and behaviors in relationships.** Encourage them to think about how they can improve and what attitudes they need to cultivate to build stronger connections.

  - **Example:** Ask open-ended questions like, "How did you feel about the way you handled that situation with your friend?" or "What do you think you could do differently next time?" This encourages self-awareness and personal growth.

- **Ineffective Example:** Criticizing your teen's behavior without offering constructive feedback or guidance, which can lead to defensiveness rather than reflection and improvement?

Teach Resilience and Patience

Help your teen understand that relationships require effort and time. Encourage them to be patient and resilient in the face of challenges.

Positive Approaches

- Share personal stories of how you overcame challenges in your relationships through patience and perseverance. Emphasize that conflicts are a natural part of relationships and can be resolved with effort and understanding.

  o Example: "In my relationship with your other parent, we've had our share of disagreements. But by being patient and working through our differences, we've become stronger as a couple."

Inadequate Approach

- Fostering a "quick fix" mentality where your teen expects immediate resolution to conflicts without putting in the necessary effort. This can lead to frustration and failed relationships.

  o Example: "Just apologize quickly and move on; it's not a big deal."

6. The Importance of Not Rushing into Sex

Rushing into sexual activity can have significant emotional, physical, and psychological consequences for teenagers. It is crucial for parents to guide their teens to make informed and deliberate decisions about sex. This guidance begins with open, honest, and ongoing communication, which helps teens develop a healthy understanding of sexuality and relationships.

The Role of Communication

Studies have shown that teenagers who have regular, meaningful conversations with their parents about sex are more likely to delay sexual activity. According to research by the National Campaign to Prevent Teen and Unplanned Pregnancy (2016), parents who communicate well with their children tend to delay their teens' initiation into sex. Conversely, 1 in 3 teenagers who do not communicate with their parents about sex are more likely to rush into sexual activity. This statistic underscores the vital role of parental involvement in their children's sexual decision-making processes.

Continuous Dialogue

The sex talk should not be a one-time event. Instead, it should be an ongoing dialogue that evolves as the child grows. Discussing sex openly and age-appropriately from an early age helps demystify the subject and provides teens with accurate information. This continuous conversation builds a foundation of trust and comfort, making teens more likely to approach their parents with questions and concerns.

Practical Guides for Parents

1. Start Early and Keep the Conversation Going

- **Effective Approach:** Begin discussing basic concepts about bodies and boundaries from a young age. As your child grows, gradually introduce more complex topics related to sex and relationships.

  - o **Example:** "Our bodies are amazing, and it's important to know how to take care of them and respect others."

- **Ineffective Approach:** Avoiding the topic entirely until your child is a teenager.

  - o **Example:** "You're too young to talk about this now. We'll discuss it when you're older."

2. Create a Safe Space for Open Communication

- **Effective Approach:** Encourage your teen to share their thoughts and feelings without fear of judgment. Listen actively and validate their experiences.

  - o **Example:** "I'm here to listen and support you. It's okay to ask questions about anything, including sex."

- **Ineffective Approach:** Reacting with shock or anger when your teen brings up sexual topics.

- o **Example:** "Why would you even think about that? You're too young!"

3. Provide Accurate Information

- **Good Approach:** Use reliable sources to educate your teen about the physical and emotional aspects of sex. Ensure they understand the importance of consent and safe sex practices.

  - o **Example:** "Sex is a natural part of life, but it's important to wait until you're ready and always practice safe sex."

- **Bad Approach:** Relying on myths or scare tactics to discourage sexual activity.

  - o **Example:** "If you have sex, you'll regret it for the rest of your life."

4. Discuss the Emotional Impact of Sex

- **Good Approach:** Explain how sex can affect emotional well-being and relationships. Encourage your teen to consider their feelings and the potential consequences before engaging in sexual activity.

  - o **Example:** "Sex can create strong emotional bonds, and it's important to be sure you're ready for that kind of connection."

- **Bad Approach:** Focusing solely on the physical risks of sex without addressing the emotional aspects.

    o **Example:** "You just need to use protection, and you'll be fine."

5. Empower Them to Make Informed Decisions

- **Good Approach:** Help your teen understand their own values and what they want in a relationship. Encourage them to set boundaries and respect those of others.

    o **Example:** "It's important to know what you want and to communicate your boundaries clearly in any relationship."

- **Bad Approach:** Making decisions for your teen without considering their perspective.

    o **Example:** "You should wait until you're married. End of discussion."

7. Recognizing Abusive Tendencies in a Relationship

Understanding and identifying abusive tendencies in a relationship is crucial for ensuring the safety and well-being of teenagers. Abusive behavior can manifest in various forms, including physical, emotional, psychological, and sexual abuse. It is vital for parents to educate their teens on how to recognize these warning signs and to empower them to seek help if needed.

Research indicates that teens who are aware of the signs of abuse are more likely to avoid or leave unhealthy relationships. According to the National Council on Crime and Delinquency Focus, 1 in 3 adolescents in the U.S. is a victim of physical, emotional, or verbal abuse from a dating partner (Love is Respect, 2021). This statistic highlights the importance of early and continuous education about abusive tendencies in relationships.

Just like the sex talk, discussions about relationship dynamics and abuse should be ongoing and adapted to the child's developmental stage. Creating an environment where teens feel comfortable discussing their relationships openly can help them recognize and avoid abusive situations.

Practical Guides for Parents

1. Start Conversations Early and Continue Them Regularly

- **Good Approach:** Introduce the concept of healthy and unhealthy behaviors in relationships from an early age. Continue to discuss these topics as your child grows.

    - **Example:** "It's important to treat everyone with kindness and respect, and to expect the same in return."

- **Bad Approach:** Avoiding the topic of abusive behavior until a problem arises.

  o **Example:** "We don't need to talk about that now; you're too young."

2. Create a Trusting and Open Environment

- **Good Approach:** Encourage your teen to talk about their relationships without fear of judgment or punishment. Be a supportive listener.

  o **Example:** "You can always talk to me about your friends and relationships. I'm here to help and support you."

- **Bad Approach:** Reacting with anger or disbelief when your teen shares concerns.

  o **Example:** "Why are you even hanging out with people like that?"

3. Educate About the Signs of Abuse

- **Good Approach:** Teach your teen the red flags of abusive behavior, such as excessive jealousy, controlling actions, and verbal insults. Ensure they know abuse can be subtle and emotional as well as physical.

- o **Example:** "If someone is trying to control who you talk to or is always criticizing you, those are signs of an unhealthy relationship."

- **Bad Approach:** Assuming your teen will recognize abusive behavior without guidance.

  - o **Example:** "You'll know if someone is bad news."

4. Encourage Self-Worth and Independence

- **Good Approach:** Help your teen build self-esteem and encourage them to pursue their interests and maintain their independence.

  - o **Example:** "You are strong and capable on your own, and you deserve to be treated with respect."

- **Bad Approach:** Discouraging independence or belittling their achievements.

  - o **Example:** "You need someone to take care of you; you can't do it all on your own."

5. Provide Resources and Support

- **Good Approach:** Ensure your teen knows where to turn for help if they find themselves in an abusive relationship. This includes talking to trusted adults and accessing community resources.

- o **Example:** "If you ever feel unsafe or unsure about a relationship, you can always come to me or contact a helpline."

- **Bad Approach:** Leaving your teen to figure it out on their own.

  - o **Example:** "You should be able to handle your own problems."

By fostering a safe and open environment, parents can help their teens recognize abusive tendencies in relationships and feel empowered to seek help. Continuous education and support are key to ensuring that teens can navigate their relationships safely and healthily.

Guiding Your Teenager Through Relationships

Guiding your teenager through the complexities of relationships is a vital aspect of their development. By providing practical advice and support in areas such as communication, conflict management, emotional regulation, resisting sexual coercion and pressure, avoiding dating violence, developing personality and character qualities, balancing attraction with values, and recognizing abusive tendencies, you can help your teen build the foundation for healthy, respectful, and fulfilling relationships. Remember, open dialogue and supportive environments are key to helping your teenager navigate these important aspects of their lives.

POINTS TO REMEMBER

The Importance of Healthy Communication

Fostering open and honest conversation with your teen increases the likelihood that they will come to you to discuss important matters, such as relationships, school, sex, and drugs, rather than turning to friends or feeling isolated. Let's begin with the most important aspect:

From Toddler
to Preadolescence

So far, I have made the case that studies confirm the importance of starting sex and relationship education early. Because Sexual development in children is a critical aspect of their overall growth and understanding of themselves. This development varies significantly with age, encompassing different behaviors, understanding, and learning stages.

2–6-year-olds

We will begin with the sexual development of children from ages 2 to preadolescence, emphasizing the importance of a healthy home environment, the role of parents, and the challenges children face at each stage.

Early Childhood (2-6 Years)

At the age of two, children begin to exhibit sexualized behaviors, reaching a peak between ages three and five. During these years, children are openly curious about their bodies and engage in exploratory behaviors such as touching their genitals or playing "doctor" with peers. This curiosity is normal and part of their physical and emotional development. According to research, these behaviors are primarily physical responses rather than actions with explicit sexual meanings.

Parents are a guide

As a Parent, we play a crucial role in this stage by guiding our children to respect their bodies and the bodies of others. It's essential to answer children's questions about their bodies calmly and directly.

For example, if a child asks why boys and girls are different, a simple explanation that boys have penises and girls have vaginas can suffice. Providing such information helps normalize their curiosity and ensures they feel comfortable discussing these topics in the future. Failing to address these questions can lead to inhibited inquiries later in life, potentially hindering their psychosexual development.

What should parents emphasize?

Boundaries

Parents should emphasize appropriate boundaries and the importance of not keeping secrets if someone violates those boundaries. This education can protect children from potential harm and exploitation. Creating an emotionally and sexually secure environment is crucial for healthy development.

Role Model

In an ideal scenario, the family is a place where children can gain a clear understanding of themselves as unique sexual beings within a secure family unit. Positive messages about sex as something natural and good, coupled with parents showing affection toward each other, help children feel secure about their parents' relationship. Parents' sexual relationships should be kept private, with clear boundaries maintained, reinforcing the concept of appropriate sexual behavior.

A major concern during this period is the exposure of children to sexualized environments, such as homes where pornography is readily available or where sexual boundaries are not respected. This exposure can undermine a child's sexual development and warp their perception of sexuality. Sexual, verbal, and physical abuse also have devastating impacts, resulting in emotional wounds that can last a lifetime. Firestone, and Catlett (2006) noted that harsh attitudes toward a child's body and developing sexuality lead to distorted views of sexuality and the human body. Parents who exploit their children to fulfill emotional or sexual needs cause significant damage, even if no sexual activity is involved.

Middle Childhood (4-11 Years)

As children grow older, their understanding of sexuality and body image evolves. Between the ages of four and six, children often begin to take on gender-stereotyped tasks, with boys engaging in more physically oriented activities and girls in nurturing roles. This scripting can influence their perceptions of gender roles and self-worth (Firestone, Firestone, & Catlett, 2006).

During the industry versus inferiority stage (ages six to eleven), boys tend to develop mastery in the external world of objects and activities, while girls often excel in social and nurturing tasks.

What should parents emphasize?

Where babies come from

It is also during this stage that parents should start discussing the basics of sexual education with their children. Simple conversations about where babies come from, the differences between boys and girls, and the concept of consent can be introduced. Using age-appropriate language is crucial. For example, explaining that a baby grows in a mother's womb and is born when the mother and father decide they want to have a child can be sufficient for younger children.

Boundaries

Parents should also address the concept of private versus public behaviors. Children need to understand that certain activities, such as touching their private parts, are appropriate only in private settings. This understanding helps establish boundaries and respect for their own and others' bodies. For instance, a parent might explain, "You might want to check whether things is right or wrong in your private part, It's okay to touch your private parts when you're alone in your room or the bathroom, but not when you're around other people."

Parents should be mindful of reinforcing these stereotypes and instead encourage a balance. For instance, boys should be encouraged to engage in nurturing activities, and girls should be affirmed in their physical and intellectual pursuits.

In a healthy home environment, children learn about sexuality as a positive and natural part of life. Parents showing affection toward each other and discussing sex positively help children feel secure about their bodies and relationships.

Encouraging questions and providing truthful answers helps build a foundation of trust.

Preadolescence (7-12 Years)

Preadolescence is marked by significant changes as children's bodies and hormones begin to change. During this stage, children often become more modest and private about their bodies. While sexual play may decline, children still exhibit interest in sexuality, albeit more discreetly.

Joan Atwood (2006) highlights that preadolescence is a time when children, particularly girls, are well-versed in sexual terms and behaviors, often unbeknownst to their parents. This period can be challenging for parents as children become more influenced by media and peer interactions.

Parents must create a safe place

Parents must create a safe and open environment for discussions about sexuality, gender, and relationships. Warm, affectionate, and caring parental relationships provide a secure foundation for children to ask questions and express their feelings. Fathers, in particular, play a vital role in their daughters' sexual development by affirming their femininity and providing emotional support.

It's also essential to address exaggerated gender stereotypes that can limit children's emotional and social development. Encouraging boys to express sensitivity and gentleness and affirming girls as strong and assertive can lead to more balanced and healthy adults. For example, boys should be taught that showing emotions is not a sign of weakness, and girls should be encouraged to participate in sports and other competitive activities without fear of being labeled "tomboys."

During this period, the media's influence becomes more pronounced. Children are exposed to various messages about gender roles, relationships, and sexuality through television, internet, and social media.

Teaching moments

Parents need to be proactive in monitoring and discussing these messages with their children. For example, if a child sees an advertisement that objectifies women, parents can discuss why this portrayal is inappropriate and how it does not reflect reality.

Additionally, parents should provide age-appropriate information about the physical changes associated with puberty. Boys and girls should understand what to expect as their bodies begin to develop secondary sexual characteristics. This education can help reduce anxiety and confusion about these changes. For instance, parents can explain that girls will start to develop breasts and may begin menstruating, while boys will experience growth in their genitals and voice changes.

Discussing the concept of consent and respectful relationships is also crucial during this stage. Children should understand that they have the right to say no to any unwanted touch or attention and that they should always respect others' boundaries.

Creating a Positive Home Environment

A positive home environment is fundamental to healthy sexual development. Children should feel safe, respected, and loved. Parents must model healthy relationships and open communication about sexuality. This foundation helps children develop a healthy self-concept and understanding of sexuality.

Exposing children to a sexualized environment where pornography is readily available and sexual boundaries are disrespected undermines their development. Such environments can warp a child's understanding of sexuality and lead to harmful behaviors and attitudes. It's essential to create an environment where healthy sexual development is supported and inappropriate influences are minimized.

Firestone, Firestone, and Catlett (2006) emphasize that harsh attitudes toward a child's body and developing sexuality lead to distorted views of sexuality and the human body. Positive reinforcement and respectful attitudes towards children's bodies and sexuality are vital. Parents should celebrate their children's milestones and affirm their bodies as beautiful and worthy of respect.

Additional role of parents

The Role of Parents in Guiding Sexual Development

Parents play an irreplaceable role in their children's sexual development. Their attitudes, behaviors, and communication styles significantly influence how children perceive and understand sexuality. Creating a warm, affectionate, and open family environment is crucial.

Open communication about sexuality should begin early and continue through adolescence. Parents should seize teachable moments to discuss various aspects of sexuality, including consent, boundaries, and respect. For example, if a child witnesses a public display of affection, a parent can explain that such behavior is appropriate in certain contexts but should be kept private in others.

Modeling

Parents should also model healthy relationships. Demonstrating respect, affection, and communication within their relationship sets a positive example for children. When children see their parents resolving conflicts healthily and respectfully, they learn important lessons about managing their own relationships.

Affirming each child's unique qualities and encouraging a broad range of interests and activities helps prevent rigid gender stereotypes. Boys should be encouraged to express emotions and engage in nurturing activities, while girls should be affirmed in their physical and intellectual pursuits. This approach fosters a balanced view of masculinity and femininity, allowing children to develop into well-rounded individuals.

Addressing Challenges and Concerns

Despite parents' best efforts, challenges and concerns will inevitably arise in their children's sexual development. Understanding common issues and how to address them can help parents navigate these challenges effectively.

One common concern is children's exposure to inappropriate content, such as pornography or explicit materials on the internet. With the prevalence of digital media, it is increasingly challenging to shield children from such content. Parents should use parental controls on devices and have open discussions about the content they may encounter online. Explaining why certain materials are inappropriate and how they can affect their perception of sex and relationships is essential. For instance, parents might say, "Some things on the internet show people in ways that are not real or respectful. If you see something that makes you uncomfortable or you have questions about, please talk to me."

Another concern is peer pressure and the influence of friends. As children grow older, they may face pressure from peers to conform to certain behaviors or beliefs about sex and relationships. Open communication about peer pressure and encouraging children to think critically about their values can help them make informed decisions. Parents can role-play scenarios with their children to help them practice standing up for their beliefs and making choices that align with their values.

Bullying related to sexual development or orientation is another issue that can arise. Children who are perceived as different may be targeted by their peers. Parents should foster an environment of acceptance and teach their children to respect diversity. If a child experiences bullying, it's crucial to take it seriously, support them, and work with school officials to address the issue. Parents can say, "Everyone is unique, and it's important to respect those differences. If someone is bullying you, it's not your fault, and we need to tell someone who can help."

Sexual abuse is a grave concern that parents must address proactively. Teaching children about body autonomy, appropriate boundaries, and how to recognize and report inappropriate behavior is essential. Reinforcing that they should never keep secrets about uncomfortable or harmful situations and ensuring they know they will be believed and supported is crucial. For example, parents can tell their children, "Your body belongs to you. If anyone touches you in a way that makes you feel uncomfortable, you should tell me or another trusted adult immediately."

The onset of puberty can bring about confusion and anxiety for children. Parents should provide accurate information about the physical and emotional changes that occur during puberty. For boys, this includes discussing changes like voice deepening, genital growth, and nocturnal emissions. For girls, it involves explaining menstruation, breast development, and other bodily changes. Using educational resources like books or videos can help make these conversations more comfortable and informative. A parent might explain, "Your body is going through changes that prepare you for adulthood. These changes are normal and happen to everyone, but if you have any questions or feel worried, you can always talk to me."

Supporting Healthy Sexual Development

Creating a supportive environment for healthy sexual development involves continuous effort and education. Parents should strive to stay informed about issues related to children's sexual development and seek resources to enhance their understanding and ability to communicate with their children effectively.

Engaging in community resources such as parenting workshops, sexual education classes, and counseling can provide additional support and information. These resources can offer guidance on discussing difficult topics, addressing concerns, and fostering a positive and open environment at home. Parents can seek out books, websites, and organizations dedicated to healthy sexual development for both themselves and their children.

Modeling healthy relationships is a powerful tool for teaching children about respect, love, and intimacy. Children learn a great deal by observing their parents' interactions. Demonstrating kindness, respect, and healthy conflict resolution sets a positive example. Additionally, parents should discuss their values and expectations regarding relationships and sexuality with their children. This dialogue helps children understand their family's values and how to incorporate them into their own lives.

Promoting body positivity and self-esteem is crucial. Children should be encouraged to appreciate their bodies and understand that everyone develops at their own pace. Parents can help by praising their children's strengths, encouraging physical activity, and promoting healthy eating habits. Positive reinforcement and avoiding negative comments about weight or appearance foster a healthy body image. Parents can remind their children, "Your body is amazing just the way it is. It's important to take care of it by eating well, staying active, and loving yourself."

Addressing media influences is also vital. Parents should actively monitor the media their children consume and discuss the messages being portrayed. This includes television shows, movies, music, and advertisements. Encouraging critical thinking about these messages and discussing the difference between media portrayals and real-life relationships can help children develop a healthy understanding of sexuality. For example, parents can watch a movie with their child and then discuss the relationships depicted, asking questions like, "Do you think that was a healthy way to handle that situation? Why or why not?"

Social and emotional aspect

Parents should also prepare their children for the social and emotional aspects of relationships. Discussing topics such as consent, mutual respect, and communication helps children understand the importance of healthy relationships. Role-playing different scenarios can provide children with the tools to navigate social situations effectively. For instance, parents can practice with their child how to say no respectfully but firmly or how to express their feelings in a relationship.

Lastly, providing continuous support and being approachable is crucial. Children should know that they can turn to their parents with any questions or concerns about sexuality and relationships. Maintaining an open door policy and responding to inquiries without judgment or discomfort fosters a trusting relationship. Parents should remind their children regularly, "You can always talk to me about anything. I'm here to help you and support you no matter what."

Conclusion

Understanding and supporting children's sexual development from early childhood through preadolescence is crucial for their overall well-being. Parents play a pivotal role in guiding their children through these stages by creating a secure and open environment for discussing sexuality. By addressing gender stereotypes, fostering healthy attitudes towards sex and relationships, and addressing common challenges and concerns, parents can help their children develop into well-rounded and confident individuals.

As children grow, they will encounter various influences and challenges related to their sexual development. Parents who remain involved, informed, and supportive can help their children develop a healthy understanding of their bodies, relationships, and sexuality. By fostering an environment of trust, respect, and open communication, parents can guide their children towards becoming well-adjusted, self-aware, and empathetic adults.

POINTS TO REMEMBER

Creating a supportive environment for healthy sexual development involves continuous effort and education. Parents should strive to stay informed about issues related to children's sexual development

Further Techniques for Parents

1. **Reflective Listening**: When your child shares something, repeat it back to show understanding and clarify their meaning. For instance, if they mention hearing about kissing at school, respond with, "It sounds like you learned something new today. What did you hear about kissing?"

2. **Ask Open-ended Questions**: Instead of yes/no questions, encourage your child to share more by asking open-ended questions. For example, instead of asking, "Do you know how babies are made?" you could ask, "Can you tell me what you know about how babies are made?"

3. **Empathize**: Validate your child's feelings and experiences to create a supportive environment. For instance, if they express confusion about something they heard, respond with, "It's understandable to feel confused when you hear something new. Let's talk about it together."

4. **Avoid Judgment**: Create a safe, judgment-free zone where your child feels comfortable expressing themselves. If they share something surprising or contrary to your beliefs, respond with curiosity rather than criticism to encourage further discussion.

5. **Encourage Further Exploration**: After your child shares, invite them to ask questions or share more if they wish. For example, you

could say, "That's interesting. Is there anything else you're curious about?"

6. **Respect Their Pace:** Be patient and allow your child to discuss topics at their own pace. Let them know you're available to talk whenever they're ready.

7. **Use Active Listening Techniques:** Show engagement through non-verbal cues like nodding and maintaining eye contact. Paraphrase what your child says to ensure understanding.

8. **Be Present:** Give your child your undivided attention during conversations about sex education. Minimize distractions such as phones to demonstrate your focus.

9. **Normalize Conversations:** Make sex education a regular topic so your child feels comfortable raising questions or concerns at any time.

10. **Follow Their Lead:** Let your child guide the conversation based on their interests and curiosity. Stay flexible to keep the discussion relevant and engaging for them.

- "What does it mean to feel loved and safe? How can we show love and kindness to others?"

- "Can you think of different ways people's bodies look? How do you feel about the differences in people's sizes, shapes, and colors?"

- "Do you know that boys and girls have different body parts? Can you tell me what you know about the differences between boys and girls?"

- "Why is it important to respect our own bodies? What are some things we can do to keep our bodies safe and healthy?"

- "Do you know the names of all the parts of your body? Can you tell me the correct names for your private parts and why it's important to know them?"

- "How do you feel when we talk about our private parts? Is it okay to talk about them without feeling naughty? Why or why not?"

- "Have you heard that it's normal to touch your private parts? Why do you think some people might do that? How can we make sure we do it in a safe and private way?"

- "Do you know how babies are born? Can you tell me what you know about how a baby gets into a woman's body and how it comes out?"

- "Do you know that not everyone has to have a baby? Why do you think some people choose to have babies and others do not?"

- "Who are the trusted adults you can talk to if you have questions or concerns about your body or feelings? How can you start a conversation with them if you need to?"

- "What would you do if someone tries to touch you in a way that makes you uncomfortable? How can you say 'NO' and get help from a trusted adult?"

About the Author

D r. Kwame Frimpong, Ph.D., is a Licensed Professional Counselor (LPC), Marriage and Family Therapist (MFT), and Nationally Certified Counselor (NCC). With over three decades of marriage and raising three adult children, Dr. Frimpong brings a wealth of personal and professional experience to his work. He is an Associate Professor of Clinical Counseling at Pentecostal Theological Seminary in Tennessee, where he educates future counselors and ministers on overcoming trauma and restoring relationships.

As an author of eight books including "Finding Him and Finding Her" A Practical Steps for Christian Dating", "Does Physical Attraction Matter", "21 Red Flags You Must Not Ignore While Dating", "9 Easy Steps To Address Red Flags", "The healing of the heart", "Overcoming Offenses", "It's Not Your Fault", Breaking Through to the Real You""15 Laws of Breakthrough", "Eat the colors Stop the

killers". He founded the former national TV ministry host on The Word Network, Dr. Frimpong is committed to helping individuals overcome broken relationships and past trauma. His workshops and research focus on the critical link between relationship health and mental health, and he passionately believes that healing in relationships fosters overall mental well-being.

After graduating from Liberty University in 2022 with a Ph.D. in Counselor Education and Supervision, Dr. Frimpong's story of faith and overcoming childhood adversity was featured in the university's graduation highlights. His journey continues to inspire, and his image has been used in Liberty University's marketing materials as a testament to his dedication to living as a Champion for Christ.

To learn more, visit his website at www.kfllifecoaching.com and www.LetsLoveRight.com

References

Advocates for Youth: www.advocatesforyouth.org

Below Your Belt: Conversations with HEART: www.bybconversations.com

HEART Women & Girls: www.heartwomenandgirls.org

Abbey, A., et al. (2014). "Sexual coercion in romantic relationships: A growing concern."

Ahern, N. R., & Mechling, B. (2013). Sexting: Serious problems for youth. *Journal of Psychological Nursing, 51* (7), 22-30.

Ahern, N. R., & Mechling, B. (2013). Sexting: Serious problems for youth. *Journal of Psychological Nursing, 51* (7), 22-30.

American Study (2008). "Violence in intimate relationships among American youth."

Australian Bureau of Statistics Data Summary 2021—Mindframe. Available online: https://mindframe.org.au/suicide/data-statistics/abs-data-summary-2021-2 (accessed on 9 March 2023).

Australian Communications and Media Authority Annual Report; Australia, 2013–2014. Available online: https://www.acma. gov.au/publications/2014-09/report/ACMA-annual-report-2013-14 (accessed on 9 March 2023).

Ayoade, C., 2006. *Relationships among leisure, social self-image, peer pressure andat-risk behaviour of adolescents in Nigeria,* University of Ilorin: An unpublished Ph.D thesis.

Ballard, C., & Morris, M. (1998). Peer influences on adolescent sexual behavior. Journal of Adolescent Research, 13(2), 122-148.

Balswick, O. J.,& Balswick, K. J. (1989). The family: A Christian perspective on the contemporary home. Grand Rapids, MI.

Benbouriche, M., & Parent, G. (2018). "Understanding the dynamics of sexual coercion."

Bonell, C., Allen, E., Strange, V., Oakley, A., Copas, A., Johnson, A., & Stephenson, J. (2006). Influence of family type and parenting behaviors on teenage sexual behavior and conceptions. *Journal of Epidemiology & Community Health, 60,* 502-506.

Bradner, C., Ku, L., & Lindberg, L. (2000). Older, but not wiser: How men get information about AIDS and sexually transmitted diseases after high school. Family Planning Perspectives, 32(1), 33-38.

Butler, C. T. (1991). *Holman Bible dictionary.* Nashville, Tenn.: Holman Bible Publishers.

Center for Disease Control (CDC) (2020). "Violence among dating adolescent couples."

Davis, T., & Harris, M. B. (1982). Sexual knowledge, sexual interests, and sources of sexual information of rural and urban adolescents from three cultures. Adolescence, 17(65), 197-209.

DeFranza, K. M. (2012). The meaning of sex: Christian ethics and the moral Life.

DiIorio, C., Kelley, M., & Hockenberry-Eaton, M. (1999). Communication about sexual issues: Mothers, fathers, and friends. Journal of Adolescent Health, 24(3), 181-189.

Downie, J., & Coates, R. (1999). The impact of school sex education on the sexual attitudes and behavior of young people. Health Education Research, 14(2), 247-256.

Emadi, S. (2013). A Review Of Justin Lee, torn: rescuing the gospel from gays-Vs.-Christians debate, *Journal for Biblical Manhood and Womanhood*, JBMW 18:2. Retrieved from. http://www.galaxie.com.ezproxy.liberty.edu/article/jbmw18-2-11?highlight=Emadi

eSafety Commissioner; Safer Internet Day 2021. Available online: https://www.esafety.gov.au/newsroom/whats-on/safer- internet-day-2021 (accessed on 9 March 2023).

Esere, M., 2008. Effect of Sex Education Programme on at-risk sexual behaviour of school-going adolescents in Ilorin, Nigeria. *Afr Health Sci,* 2(8), pp. 120-125..

Flood, M. (2007). Exposure to pornography among youth in Australia. *Journal of Sociology, 43* (1), 45-60.

Ford, K., & Norris, A. E. (1991). Urban African-American and Hispanic adolescents and young adults: Relationship of STD, AIDS, and HIV knowledge to actual risk. Journal of Youth and Adolescence, 20(3), 179-191.

French, B. H., et al. (2015). "Psychological and physical coercion in adolescent dating relationships."

Glowacz, F., et al. (2018). "Alcohol and drug use in sexual coercion among adolescents."

Hacker KA. Listening to youth: teen perspectives on pregnancy prevention. Journal of Adolescent Health 2000; 26(4): 279-88.

Hembach, R. D. (2007). Schaeffer on sex today. *Faith and Mission, FM 24:2.* Retrieved from http://www.galaxie.com.ezproxy.liberty.edu/article/fm24-2-06.

Holtzman, D., & Rubinson, R. (1995). Parent and peer communication effects on AIDS-related behavior among U.S. high school students. Family Planning Perspectives, 27(6), 235-240.

Houck, C., Swenson, R., Donenberg, G., Papino, A., Emerson, E., & Brown, L. K. (2014). Adolescents' emotions prior to sexual activity and association with sexual risk factors. *Journal of AIDS and Behavior, 18*, 1615-1623.

Hughes, R. D. (2014). The internet pornography pandemic: The largest unregulated social experiment in human history. *Christian Apologetics Journal,* CAJ 12:1. Retrieve from http://www.galaxie.com.ezproxy.liberty.edu/article/caj12-1-03?highlight=effect%20of%20pornography.

Hyde, J., & DeLamater, J. (2017). *Understanding human sexuality* (13th ed.). New York, NY: McGraw-Hill.

Ikenberry, G.J.; Smith, A.D. Myths and Memories of the Nation. *Foreign Aff.* **2000**, *79*, 149. [CrossRef]

Inc. New Strategist Publications. (2006). Teenage sexual activity. In Inc. New Strategies Publications (Ed.), *American sexual behavior* (pp. 33-51). Amityville, NY: Editor.

Jewell D, Tacchi J, Donovan J. Adolescents from different socioeconomic back- grounds had different attitudes about teen pregnancy. *Evidence-Based Nursing*, 2000: 4: 125. 63

Jones, W. D. (2004) The asperity of sexual sin: exploring the sexual-spiritual nexus, Faith and Mission,FM 22:1. Retrieved from. http://www.galaxie.com.ezproxy.liberty.edu/article/fm22-1-01?highlight=The%20Asperity%20of%20Sexual%20Sin

Journal of Interpersonal Violence (2022). "Adolescents' relationships and violence."

Kaiser Family Foundation. (2005). Sexual Health Statistics for Teenagers in the United States. Henry J. Kaiser Family Foundation.

Karofsky PS et al. Relationship between adolescent parental communication and initiation of first intercourse by adolescents. Journal of Adolescent Health 2000: 28; 41-45

King, B. M., & Lorusso, J. (1997). Discussions of sexual issues with young children: Parents' attitudes and practices. Child Study Journal, 27(2), 105- 121.

Kirwil, L. Parental Mediation of Children's Internet Use In Different European Countries. *J. Child. Media* **2009**, *3*, 394–409.

Lim, K.H.; Leung, K.; Sia, C.L.; Lee, M.K.O. Is eCommerce boundary-less? Effects of individualism–collectivism and uncertainty avoidance on Internet shopping. *J. Int. Bus. Stud.* **2004**, *35*, 545–559.

Livingston, J. A. (2022). "The impact of maternal relationships on adolescent dating violence."

Livingstone, S.; Sefton-Green, J. The Class: Living and Learning in the Digital Age. *Eur. J. Commun.* **2017**, *32*, 185. [CrossRef]

Love is Respect. (2021). Dating Abuse Statistics. Retrieved from https://www.loveisrespect.org/resources/dating-violence-statistics/

Maduakonam, A., 2001. Sex education in schools: A panacea for adolescent sexuality Problems.. In: O. R. e. In: Okonkwo RUN, ed. *The Nigerian Adolescent In Perspective..* Akwa: Theo Onwuka and Sons Publishers, p. 74–82

McCulloch A. Teenage childbearing in Great Britain and the spatial concentration of poverty households. *J of Epidemiol Community Health*, 2000: **55**: 16–23.

McKee, A. (2010). Does pornography harm young people? *Australian Journal of Communication, 37*(1), 17-36.

Miller, K. S., Kotchick, B. A., Dorsey, S., Forehand, R., & Ham, A. Y. (1998). Family communication about sex: What are parents saying and are their adolescents listening? Family Planning Perspectives, 30(5), 218-222.

Ministry of Women's Empowerment and Child Protection (2022). "Annual report on sexual violence."

Ministry of Women's Empowerment and Child Protection (2022). "Cases of sexual violence in Indonesia."

Mohler. A. R. (2015). We Cannot Be Silent: Speaking Truth to a Culture Redefining Marriage, Sex, and the Very Meaning of Right and Wrong. Journal for Biblical Manhood and Womanhood, JBMW 20:2. Retrieved from. http://www.galaxie.com.ezproxy.liberty.edu/article/jbmw20-2-12?highlight=mohler%202015

National Campaign to Prevent Teen and Unplanned Pregnancy. (2016). Parental Influence on Teen Sexual Behavior: A Guide for Parents.

National Council on Crime and Delinquency Focus. (n.d.). Adolescent Victimization.

Nolin, M. J., & Petersen, D. M. (1992). Gender differences in parents' attempts to discuss sexual topics with adolescents. Journal of Adolescent Research, 7(1), 59-79.

Nwabuisi, E., 2004. *Support networks and adjustment needs of HIV/AIDS patients in the Zonal 'hotspots' in Nigeria,* University of Ilorin: An unpublished Ph. D Thesis

Ott MA, Pfeiffer EJ. "That's nasty" to curiosity: early adolescent cognitions about sexual abstinence. J Adolesc Health 2009 Jun;44(6):575-581 [FREE Full text] [doi: 10.1016/j.jadohealth.2008.10.139] [Medline: 19465322]

Patton GC, Sawyer SM, Santelli JS, Ross DA, Afifi R, Allen NB, et al. Our future: a Lancet commission on adolescent health and wellbeing. Lancet 2016 Jun 11;387(10036):2423-2478 [FREE Full text] [doi: 10.1016/S0140-6736(16)00579-1] [Medline: 27174304]

Pazol K et al. Vital Signs: Teen Pregnancy — United States, 1991–2009. MMWR, April 2011.

Penner, J. J., & Penner, C. L. (2005). *Counseling for sexual disorders.* Pasadena, CA: Piper, J. (2012). Let marriage be held in honor— Thinking Biblically about so-called same-sex marriage. *Journal for Biblical Manhood and Womanhood, JBMW 17:2* . Retrieved from http://www.galaxie.com.ezproxy.liberty.edu/article/jbmw17-2-06?highlight=let%20marriage%20be%20held%20in%20honor

Priscilla Papers. PP 26:4. Retrieved *from.*

  http://www.galaxie.com.ezproxy.liberty.edu/article/pp26-4-
  07?highlight=Defranza

Proeve, M., & Reilly, E. (2007). Personal and offending characteristics
  of child sexual offenders who have been sexually abused.
  Psychiatry, Psychology and Law, 14(2), 251+. Retrieved from
  http://ezproxy.liberty.edu/login?url=http://go.galegroup.com.ezpr
  oxy.liberty.edu/ps/i.do?p=ITOF&sw=w&u=vic_liberty&v=2.1&it=
  r&id=GALE%7CA171771004&sid=summon&asid=32efaf73fe30c55
  590f3d84a5570bd27

Remafedi, G., 1999. Predictors of unprotected intercourse among gay
  and bisexual youth: knowledge, beliefs, and behavior.. *Pediatrics,* p.
  163–168.

Resnick, M. (1997). Protecting Adolescents from harm: Findings from
  National Longitudinal Study on Adolescent Health. JAMA,
  278:823-32

Rosenthal, D. A., & Feldman, S. S. (1999). The importance of
  importance: Adolescent perceptions of parental communication
  about sexuality. Journal of Adolescence, 22(6), 835-851.

Schwartz, S.J.; Côté, J.E.; Arnett, J.J. Identity and Agency in Emerging
  Adulthood. *Youth Soc.* 2005, *37*, 201–229. [CrossRef]

Scott, H.; Biello, S.M.; Woods, H.C. Social media use and adolescent sleep patterns: Cross-sectional findings from the UK millennium cohort study. *BMJ Open* **2019**, *9*, e031161. [CrossRef] [PubMed]

Selwyn, N. Minding our language: Why education and technology is full of bullshit... and what might be done about it. *Learn. Media Technol.* **2015**, *41*, 437–443.

Shrock, D. (2014). "True sexual morality:" An interview with Daniel Heimbach, Journal for Biblical Manhood and Womanhood, JBMW 19:1. Retrieved from http://www.galaxie.com.ezproxy.liberty.edu/article/jbmw19-1-03?highlight=David%20Schrock%202014.

Stern, H. D. (1989). *Jewish new testament commentary.* Clarksville, MD: Jewish new testament publications.

Stewart, T. J. (2003). The Biblical theology regarding homosexuality, Faith and Mission. FM 20:3. Retrieved from. http://www.galaxie.com.ezproxy.liberty.edu/article/fm20-3-02?highlight=STEWART%202003

Testa, M., & Dermen, K. H. (1999). "Alcohol consumption and its effects on sexual coercion."

Tucker, J. S., Fitzmaurice, A. E., Imamura, M., Penfold, S., Penney, G. C., Teijlingen, E., Shucksmith, J., & Philip K. L. (2006). The effect of the national demonstration project *healthy respect* on teenage

sexual health behavior. *European Journal of Public Health, 17*(1),

33-41.Retrieved from:

http://www.gospelway.com/morality/sexual_cohabitation.php
Retrieved from:

http://www.prophecynewswatch.com/2014/January31/315.html

Tulviste, T.; Ahtonen, M. Child-Rearing Values of Estonian and
Finnish Mothers and Fathers. *J. Cross-Cult. Psychol.* **2007**, *38*, 137–155. [CrossRef]

Wight D, Fullerton D. A review of interventions with parents to
promote the sexual health of their children. *Journal of Adolescent Health.* 2013;52(1):4–27. [PubMed] [Google Scholar]

Made in the USA
Columbia, SC
09 February 2025

53137632R00115